The Business Playbook

A Guide for Jamaican Startups

Written by

Christine McLean

In collaboration with

This book is dedicated to my mom, may I inherit even half her strength, and to those who dream about starting a business. It is time to make that dream real.

Table of Contents

Foreword

The Business Playbook is about business and entrepreneurship. These two concepts have been lost in a fog of mystery for many years for the Micro Small and Medium-Sized Enterprise (MSME) sector. They were postulated as concepts for big companies while MSMEs were "doing a ting", maybe based on failed attempts to get that elusive job.

The readers of this book should see that conceptualising a business, and implementing it successfully, is really a logical and rational step by step process. The book takes the process from an ivory tower to put it where it belongs – within reach of everyone who chooses to establish a business instead of seeking a job.

This book is about the ability to dream (vision). It inspires readers to use a logical, structural approach to develop the courage to persevere and ensure that one of the main ingredients is always at the heart of things – passion.

Congratulations to Ms. McLean for her contribution in changing the perception of business and entrepreneurship through the presentation of detailed information on the "main roads" of the journey, the "side roads" and also the "detours" that might be encountered along the journey.

Much success for this book is anticipated.

Valerie Veira CD, JP

Introduction

Start a business and you will hit the jackpot! At least that is what many people think. A business can be a sure way to financial freedom but getting there is not easy. This guide takes you through the steps that you need to take if you want to start, fund and maintain a healthy business in Jamaica.

Do you want to find a business idea? This guide will help you do that. Do you want to know the legal requirements to set up your business? This guide will shine a light on that. Are you looking for financing? This guide will point you in the right direction. Do you want to know how to take your business to the next level? This guide will provide you with some tips to get there.

This guide is meant to be the complete package for those who want to start a small business in Jamaica. It is refreshing to have all the information you need in one place. Gone are the days when you would have to run around like a headless chicken trying to figure out what you need to do to set up your business the *right* way.

Starting a business is like playing a game of chess. Success is more likely if you know the right strategies. Think of this guide as your playbook for the business chess game. You will learn how to:

- Identify the right business idea for you
- Develop your business idea so that it has a better chance of success
- Register your business at the Companies Office of Jamaica and file annual returns
- File business taxes and other statutories
- Find local agencies that offer business support
- Create a solid financial plan
- Step up your networking
- Develop a marketing strategy to take your sales to another level
- Develop the soft skills needed to be a successful entrepreneur in Jamaica

Jamaica has a growing micro, small and medium sized enterprise (MSME) sector. The chess board is open. Are you ready to get in the game?

Chapter One: *Creep Before Yuh Walk*

"Yuh can cook good man. Wah mek yuh nuh open wah cook shop?" Chances are you have heard this question before if you are Jamaican. Most Jamaicans have at least one friend or family member who cooks really well and we believe that skill is enough to open a successful cook shop (restaurant). The reality is that being a skilled cook does not necessarily mean that you will be a successful cook shop owner. Skill is only a small ingredient in the sizzling pot of entrepreneurship.

The same is true for any skill imaginable. You could be a skilled diva, dancehall queen, dancer, hair stylist… skill is only a small part of what you need to succeed as a Jamaican entrepreneur. I am amazed daily by the number of similar businesses in my small hometown, Mandeville. Locals seem to believe that their skills revolve around one or more of the following types of businesses: clothing store, car mart, cook shop, shipping company, supermarket or variety store. Those who live in Mandeville know that it is one of the most difficult markets to break into in Jamaica. Do we really need another car mart when there are already five others?

Our country needs fresh business ideas that can propel growth. We live in a world where there is nothing new under the sun; coming up with a truly unique business idea is difficult. However, it is not impossible. There are five critical principles that you should learn before you jump at the first business idea you conceive. These principles form a complete picture of everything you need to become a successful entrepreneur.

Dare to be different.

Doing what everyone else is doing will not work in the long-term. It is a form of insanity and Albert Einstein defined insanity as, "Doing the same thing over and over again, but expecting different results." Establishing a business that is essentially the same as existing companies means that you will ultimately use only price to compete. Sure, Jamaicans search for the best deal on everything (that's why Chiney shops are so popular). However, creating a unique business that meets an unmet need in the market in an affordable way has a greater chance of sustainable success.

I recently happened upon a former high school batchmate who is a prime example of the value of being unique. He is passionate about fitness and had been paying a small fee to train people at his friend's gym. His clients loved him so, when the gym closed, his phone was ringing constantly with personal training requests. He had to shift gears. This was going to be a big risk, but he invested close to $200,000 in portable gym equipment and scheduled in-home personalized training sessions with his loyal clients.

Little did he know that the demand would be so great. Word quickly spread and he now has more clients than he can handle. Despite the spike, his challenge has been maintaining consistency. Clients will cancel at the last minute and he does not feel that the income stream is secure enough to warrant leaving his full-time job just yet. He is working on solving this challenge. Nevertheless, his passion for fitness has helped him create what can potentially grow into a lucrative business.

Know your market.

My batchmate's experience illustrates an important point. He believed that his clients loved his service so much that they would be willing to pay for in-home personal training. There was a need that he could fill in a unique way. Being a personal trainer is nothing new but providing personalised in-home training is rare in Jamaica. The result could have been different if his clients preferred the gym experience. He paid keen attention to what the market was demanding and adjusted accordingly.

Too often, we create businesses based on what we *think* the market wants. We also have those one or two friends or family members who boost our egos and tell us that we are the best thing since sliced bread. Remember that skill is one thing but what the market demands is another.

Let me make it clear. I am not suggesting that you should not open a restaurant if you're a skilled cook. In other words, I am not telling you to ignore your skill. Your talents and abilities help considerably when building a business. However, you need to pay attention to your market. How many other restaurants are there in the vicinity? What do people like about these restaurants? How will yours be different? It does not make sense to open just another restaurant that fails to meet the needs of the market.

This discussion brings to mind an entrepreneur who understood her market and dared to be different. She now has a successful restaurant that is a favorite chill spot for those who live in Mandeville. Have you heard of Voilá? Chef Lilee knew that Mandeville needed somewhere welcoming where people could have good food and chill. She is a trained chef and knew that she could use her skills to open a bistro-style restaurant. People love it! Be like Chef Lilee and develop a true understanding of your market.

Understand that entrepreneurship is a tough, often lonely, road.

There is a common misconception that people will be banging at your door the moment you open for business. Even entrepreneurs with in-demand products take a few months to grow to a point where people are clamoring for what they offer. Instant success stories are few and far between. It takes time to build a client base. It takes time for people to see your worth. It takes time for word-of-mouth advertising to work its magic.

I was blessed with the opportunity to feature the founder and CEO of Toddler Care Jamaica in Success Lifestyle Magazine's third issue. She started her business because she loves babies. It took *7 years* before demand for her babysitting services grew and the company became profitable. I believe her passion motivated her to stick with it despite how bleak it seemed. It also helped that there is no other business in Jamaica like hers. She carved out her niche, spent time building trust, and is quickly becoming a household name in Jamaica. Her story is a prime example of the typical cycle of business profitability; it can take 3 years for a business to **break even** and *5 years for it to be profitable*. Let that sink in.

Do not believe that you are a part of the one percent that will have an easy time building your business from scratch. You will sacrifice your time, money, and relationships as you put in the work to make your business succeed. The moment you choose to give up is the moment everything will start falling apart.

Building a business from scratch will hit your finances hard. Searching for investors will be hard because most want to see proof of sales to determine how quickly their money can be recouped. You will be using your own money for months, maybe even years, and there are times when you will hit rock bottom. Understand this reality from the get-go so that you can develop the mental dexterity to handle the challenges ahead.

You don't need a degree to start a business.

Education is important. However, it does not determine your ability to be a successful entrepreneur. In fact, those with tertiary level degrees often end up looking for jobs instead of creating their own.

Entrepreneurs have highly creative minds and a determination that knows no bounds. They understand the value of people and relationships. Leveraging their connections helps them get their feet off the ground and use their skills to build empires.

Most people already know Steve Jobs' story. However, what we tend to forget is that he did not work alone as he built the first Apple computer. He was a brilliant salesman and conceiver of ideas, but he needed the brilliant software and hardware development expertise of Steve Wozniak to create the product. You may not have the requisite knowledge for *all* elements of your business. However, you can partner with people whose strengths compensate for your weaknesses.

Smart entrepreneurs build on their capabilities through experience and networking. They also know when it is the right time to stop building alone and seek external help. It is not about having a university degree. Not having a university degree does not make you inferior.

There will be many "no's" before you get a "yes".

Rejection can be a painful experience. Entrepreneurship is riddled with rejection. Imagine this scenario. You walk into a room filled with 100 people who are there to learn more about your product. They have never heard about it before and you are slightly nervous, but also excited. You have spent months, probably even years, working on your product. In your eyes, it is perfect and you expect everyone in the room to feel the same. They won't. Some people will wonder what the hell you are talking about and why you wasted their time.

Nevertheless, there is a light at the end of the tunnel. One person loves what you presented and wants to order 10 cases for her store. You may not have convinced the other 99 people, but that 1 person has changed your world. Always remember that there is a one percent chance that someone will say yes. Keep pushing until you get that yes.

How to Find a Business Idea

The pressure to create a unique business may bring anxiety. How do you find the *right* business idea? The answer to this question is not simple. Sometimes you will think about a business idea after months of subconsciously observing a problem. Something just clicks in that moment and you develop the drive to figure out how to solve the problem.

The W-I-N strategy can also guide you towards finding a business idea; it can help inch you closer to that "aha" moment.

W- Watch, read and observe.

All businesses are created to solve a problem. How will you know the problems that exist in Jamaica if you do not know what is happening in Jamaica? Watch the news, read the Jamaica Gleaner and the Jamaica Observer, and observe what is happening in your community.

Here are some random ideas I came up with based on what has been happening in Jamaica over the past few months:

- PEP tutoring and mentoring
- Garbage collecting, compacting and recycling

- Affordable non-plastic drink containers for restaurants
- Financial literacy advocate to help the average person understand how to take advantage of the surge in IPOs
- Fun summer activities for children
- Property management as more people take advantage of the reduced Stamp Duty

These are only based on my observations. You may be able to come up with other ideas based on your observations and situations unique to your community. It is important to pay attention to current events both locally and internationally since these events can lead to business opportunities.

Global emerging trends are also important. These trends tend to be industry specific but knowing what they are can help you stay ahead of the game and create a business that has a better chance of survival. Some emerging trends that I have noticed are:

- Increasing value being placed on Artificial Intelligence (AI) as a solution to some of the world's most complex problems.
- Addressing concerns with deep sea water pollution.

- Impact investing where financial investments are made in projects that benefit the community.

- Environment preservation to mitigate the effects of climate change

- Integrating technology into real estate.

I- Identify the skills you have that can help you solve the problem.

Remember skill is only one ingredient in the sizzling pot of entrepreneurship. That does not mean that it is not important. In fact, you are at a greater advantage when you have skills relevant to the business you want to start. Otherwise, you will depend heavily on the guidance of others.

Avn Fullwood, founder of Cut Right Designs, is an example of how having the right skills can help your business grow. Her business was created out of her own need to find monogram signs for the events she coordinates for her other business, Fully Covered. She could not find what she wanted locally. So, she used her natural artistic skills to make her own signs. Little did she know that there were other people who wanted the same thing. Her business has grown exponentially, and she is constantly improving her skills to meet specific client requests.

N- Never forget to identify your competitors.

Competitor research is important for you to understand what the market is like and the value you can add. Look for similar businesses that reach your target audience. Your search should reveal the answers to these questions:

What do customers like about this brand?

What is the brand's weakness?

How is the brand reaching new customers?

What makes the brand unique?

These questions should lead to your discovering what you can do differently. If you have no competitors, then that can be a good sign. Use this as your opportunity to carve out a niche.

How Can You Find the Right Business Name?

Finding the right business name ultimately boils down to one thing: branding. In theory, there really is no right or wrong business name, but how the brand is marketed greatly impacts its recognition regardless of the business name chosen. Nevertheless, some key tips that you should consider when identifying the *right* business name include:

- Avoid offensive names. Do your research to determine if the name you have chosen is offensive in another language or culture.

- Ensure that the name is not being used by someone else. A quick search on the Companies Office of Jamaica's website and on Google can help you determine whether the name has already been used.

- Shorter names are better.

- It is a good idea to incorporate the products or services you sell in the name so that customers clearly understand what you sell, and you can improve your search engine rankings. This is not mandatory though.

- Get opinions from people you trust to be honest.

What Will You Need to Develop Your Business Idea?

You need one important tool to help you develop a business idea: a business plan. It acts as a powerful guide to direct your vision for the company and flesh out a winning business idea. Additionally, a business plan is often needed when seeking investment from financial institutions and venture capital firms.

A business plan has the following elements:

- Executive Summary
- Company Description
- Products and Services
- Market Analysis
- Organization and Management Team
- Financial Plan and Projections

Before we dive into the key elements of each section, here are some tips to help you write a strong business plan:

- Break up the text in your business plan with useful images that add value.
- Anyone should be able to read your business plan in 15 minutes or less and get a good sense of your business.
- Put detailed financial information in the appendices. Include summarised financial information in the body text.
- Write for your audience. A business plan that you are writing as a guide for yourself probably will not have as many details as a business plan you write for potential investors.

- Include proof for any claims you make.

- Use conservative financial projections.

There are some tips mentioned in each section that may not apply to you at this stage since you are only trying to develop a business idea. However, this section is detailed enough so that you can come back to it later when your business grows, and you need to revise your business plan.

Executive Summary

This section provides a bird's eye view of your business. It is short and spicy, enticing the reader to flip the page to learn more. Some key elements to include are:

- The name and address of the business

- What you sell

- Mission and vision statements

- A sentence explaining the purpose of the business plan

Company Description

Anyone reading your company description should be able to answer the following questions:

- What type of business is this? Is it a sole proprietorship, partnership, limited liability company or corporation? (We will look at the types of business structures later in this book.)

- What is the company's history?

- What industry does the business operate in?

- What is the business' unique selling position (USP)?

- What is the company's market share?

- How financially healthy is the company?

- How has the company grown?

Products and Services

Your aim at this stage is to start building a case that proves your products or services work and are needed. Some tips for writing this section include:

- A description of your products or services in the simplest possible language.

- An explanation of the value your products or services add to the customer. What problem are you solving for the customer?

- An explanation of relevant patents or copyrights issued.

- A description of how the company plans to be continuously innovative to meet the changing needs of customers and stay relevant.

Market Analysis

Market research is important for understanding the true state of the market and the customers you hope to reach. This section of the analysis can also be called your marketing strategy. It seeks to answer the question, "What will you do based on your market research?"

Do primary market research. Head to the streets and give out questionnaires. Set up focus groups. Interview random people in your target demographic. Market research is something we tend to shy away from because it is time consuming and not something introverts like to do. However, it is necessary so that you can get a true picture of the demand for your product.

Describe the competitive landscape of the industry. Who are your competitors? What is the outlook for the industry? What are the strengths and weaknesses of your competitors? What do you do differently?

Define your target customer. Some businesses suffer because they are not clear about the customers they are trying to target. Being specific helps you create successful targeted marketing campaigns. In fact, an outline of your targeted campaign(s) should be included in this section of your business plan. Think carefully about your target customers' age, income, ethnicity, location, hobbies, interests and pain points.

Organization and Management Team

The company's organization and management are important for understanding growth prospects and whether the company is well led. Here are some questions that you should answer:

- What is your operations cycle?
- Who are the members of your management team? What value do they bring?
- Who are the owners of the company?
- Who are the members of the board?
- Who are the company's advisors?

The reality is that micro businesses tend not to have teams. Nevertheless, it is important to include details about your background and experience. It helps anyone reading the business plan understand who you are and why you are capable of running this organisation.

Financial Plan and Projections

It is all about the numbers at the end of the day. You may not have any sales yet, but you can make projections based on perceived market demand. As your business grows, you can amend your projections based on actual sales figures.

Here are some elements that you should include in your amended business plan:

- Income statement, balance sheet and cash flow statement
- Forecasted income statement balance sheet and cash flow statement based on existing sales
- A ratio and trend analysis

Wow! Writing a business plan does seem rather daunting. However, there are skilled writers and business experts who can help you create the business plan you need. Contact us at info@successlifestylemagazine.com for further details.

What If you Want to Create an Online Business?

We live in a figuratively borderless world. Social media, freelancing websites, podcasts, course creator platforms and website builder sites enable us to reach customers around the world. For example, there is a Jamaican fashion designer whose main customer base is overseas clients. She receives payments via PayPal and uses our post office's express delivery system to ship goods. Her international customer base keeps her business alive.

You are not limited to a business with a physical location in Jamaica. There are more people creating online businesses now than ever before. You can enter this market if you are willing to:

- Deal with logistics issues if you are shipping products
- Invest time and money in social media marketing, email marketing and content marketing
- Build a remote team
- Work with clients in different time zones
- Work with clients who have different cultural backgrounds

Here is the stickler; an online business is not exempt from the local business registration and tax filing process. You will learn more about how to complete these stages of the business creation process later in this book.

Key Points from Chapter One

- Skill is only a small ingredient of business success.
- Finding a unique business idea takes time, but it is not impossible.
- Understanding your competitors is important; you can better understand the truly unique characteristics of your product or service.
- Primary market research provides better insight into the demand for your product or service.
- A business plan acts as a guide for fleshing out your business idea. It should be revised as your business grows and you have real data (such as sales figures).
- You can create an online business, but you should not ignore the required business registration and tax filing processes.

Checklist

- ☐ Business idea created.

- ☐ Competitors identified.

- ☐ Unique selling position identified.

- ☐ First stage business plan developed.

Reflection Question

Which of the five critical business principles mentioned in this chapter are you struggling with the most? Why?

_____

_____

_____

_____

_____

_____

_____

_____

_____

_____

_____

_____

_____

_____

_____

_____

_____

Chapter Two: *Get Legal Mi Boss*

Your business is operating illegally if it is not registered at both the Companies Office of Jamaica and the Tax Administration of Jamaica. Additionally, there are serious repercussions for businesses that do not complete the necessary follow-up action to correctly file taxes and annual returns. This chapter explains the business registration, annual return filing and tax filing processes.

Part One: The Companies Office of Jamaica

The Companies Office of Jamaica is the hub for all business registration. Jamaica's informal business sector has flown under the radar for decades because great effort has not been taken to ensure complete compliance. However, as Jamaica adopts more growth strategies to achieve the objectives of Vision 2030, greater emphasis will be placed on ensuring that *all* businesses comply with the business registration and tax compliance requirements.

33

Registering your company opens more doors of opportunity than you could access otherwise. Yuh legal now bredrin! Here are some of the things being legal can help you achieve:

- More investments
- A bank account in the company's name
- Increased consumer confidence

Not registering your business with the Companies Office of Jamaica can lead to severe consequences which include:

- Paying exorbitant fees that can go to as high as 150 percent.
- Being prosecuted for advertising. Any business that advertises must be registered.
- Losing legal battles if the defence brings up the fact that the business is unregistered.

It is important for you to stay ahead of the game by registering your business from the get-go. You identified a viable business idea in chapter one and have developed the confidence to make it a reality. It is now time for you to identify the most appropriate business structure and register your business accordingly.

Which Business Structure is Right for Me?

The Companies Office of Jamaica accommodates registration for 2 broad categories of business structures:

- Sole Proprietorship
- Corporation/ Company

Sole Proprietorship

The sole proprietorship is the simplest type of business to create. It costs less than $3,000 to register and the renewal process is done every 3 years. This business structure is ideal for:

- Freelancers
- Entrepreneurs who work alone
- Small business owners with no more than 5 employees
- Partnerships

However, there is a drawback. There is no separation between the assets of the sole proprietor and the company's assets. This means that your personal assets can be used to pay the company's debts and any money passing through your personal bank accounts is liable for audit.

Registering a sole proprietorship means that you are registering a business name. Therefore, your business will be governed under the Business Names Act. The process can either be completed online or at the Companies Office of Jamaica's physical location at 1 Grenada Way, Kingston 5.

Here are the steps to complete the process on the Companies Office of Jamaica's website:

1. Create a profile on the Companies Office of Jamaica website.
2. Go to the homepage and click "Online Services" followed by "Registration (New)".
3. You will be prompted to conduct a search of your ideal business name to see if the name is already being used. If it is not being used, you should click the option to reserve it for 90 days.
4. The portal takes you through several steps for completing the process. Pay attention to the instructions and ensure that you have scanned copies of the following documents:

- o Photo identification (driver's license, passport, or national ID)
- o Your TRN
- o Proof of address for the business. This proof should be in your name.
- o Any trade licenses or certificates for professions that require it. For instance, someone operating a food business would need a food handler's permit. Ensure that you know the necessary permits and licenses for your skill area before starting the registration process.

5. You will be prompted to pay a fee of roughly $3,000.

6. Your official business registration certificate will be available for collection within 5 business days.

You should complete the BRF V 10 5 (Super Form) Business Registration form if you are registering the company in person. This form can be downloaded from the Companies Office website or picked up at the office. You will also need to have the documents listed in step four when completing the registration process in person.

The renewal process is completed every three years. It is necessary so that the Companies Office knows that your business is still functioning and that you want to keep that business name. Keep tabs on this so that you do not miss the renewal date.

Company/Corporation

The Companies Office recognizes two types of companies:
- For-profit
- Non-profit

For-profit entities include limited liability companies (LLCs) and can also include partnerships. A partnership is better registered using the business name registration process if the business employs five persons or less. Non-profit entities include charities.

Companies are governed by the Companies Act and it costs less than $30,000 to register them. One of the greatest benefits of a company is that it is recognized as a separate entity from the people who create it. In other words, there is a clear separation between personal assets and company assets.

Non-profit companies also need to register with the Department of Co-operatives and Friendly Societies. Company registration is not facilitated on the Companies Office of Jamaica website. You should complete the BRF V 10 5 (Super Form) Business Registration form and the Articles of Incorporation (form 1A or 1B). The documents must be submitted it in-person to the Companies Office. You will need:

- The signature of 2 company directors
- Particulars of company secretary
- TRN of all directors
- Proof of business address
- Original government issued identification of the principal director and the person declaring the form's accuracy
- Relevant certification for specialist fields

Your certified business registration certificate will be available for pick-up within five business days. This certificate will include the business registration number, a number that you will need to remember as you continue to do business in Jamaica.

What Should You Do After You Have Registered at the Companies Office of Jamaica?

You may believe that you can breathe a sigh of relief after registering your business. The hard part is over, right? Reality check! There are several follow up steps that you should keep on top of to avoid financial penalties:

All businesses, whether they are sole proprietorships or companies, should be registered with the Tax Administration of Jamaica. *The business registration process is incomplete until this is done*. This process is completed at your local tax office and results in your business being assigned a TRN. The TRN for a sole proprietor is the individual's personal TRN; a company/corporation gets a separate TRN. You will also be asked to create an online account to make the tax filing process easier. Further details will be provided in the next chapter.

Additionally, you should renew your sole proprietorship business name every three years. *Annual return filings are not required for sole proprietorships.* There is a renewal of business name form that you should complete. Speak with a Companies Office of Jamaica representative for further details.

There is a process for filing annual returns for companies (both for-profit and non-profit). These forms should be completed and submitted on the anniversary of incorporation (registration). For instance, annual company returns should be filed on July 25, 2020 if you registered your company on July 25, 2019. For-profit companies should complete and submit Form 19a while non-profit companies should complete Form 19b. It costs $5,000 to file an annual return and there is a penalty for not filing within 28 days of the due date. Speak with a Companies Office of Jamaica representative for further details.

Part Two: The Tax Administration of Jamaica

April 1, 2019 is a crucial date in Jamaica's history. On this date, Santa Clarke's tax reform package took effect. Jamaicans were initially shell-shocked and excited that a substantial macroeconomic move was finally being made to stimulate the growth of the small business sector. Santa Clarke, who is really our beloved Finance Minister Nigel Clarke, created a stimulus package that arguably surpassed any other stimulus package set by his predecessors.

This tax package created a series of tax breaks that several new and existing entrepreneurs could use to their advantage.

- The threshold for filing general consumption tax (GCT) was moved from $3 million to $10 million.

- The stamp duty charge on property transfers was reduced to a flat fee of $5,000 per document for parcels representing transactions above $500,000. This is an important consideration for people purchasing real estate.

- The transfer tax rate on the sale of property was reduced from five percent to two percent.

- The minimum business tax of $60,000 was removed.

- The $100,000 asset tax on non-financial institutions was also removed.

- Business owners are required to pay taxes if their businesses fall into one or more of the following categories:
  - Revenue is $10 million or more. GCT returns must be filed in this case.
  - A self-employed person must file tax returns if annual income is greater than $1,509,600.
  - Any business with employees must pay taxes for those employees.

Dr. Clarke sweetened the deal even further in his 2020/2021 budget presentation. Two important tax benefits were mentioned for business owners. Firstly, GCT was reduced from 16.5 percent to 15 percent. Secondly, any MSME that earns less than $375,000 in profits will not pay income tax although these businesses will still be required to pay NIS, NHT and Education Tax on any income the business earns.

These updates highlight the importance of keeping abreast with the most recent changes to tax regulations. Always read the summary of each budget presentation after it has been released so that you can determine the changes that will impact your business.

Mi know. Life haad. Why should you hand over any of your hard-earned money to the government especially when corruption is rife? The simplest answer is that there are harsh penalties for tax delinquency. You can end up paying twice as much when penalties are applied or, even worse, you could be sent to prison.

Taxes finance the country. Sure, some politicians are corrupt, and it doesn't seem like that will change in the foreseeable future. However, your taxes are used for some amount of good. They are used to:

- Pay public sector workers

- Fund community projects

- Improve infrastructure

- Create job opportunities

- Fund schools

- Provide scholarships for students

The list could go on. Nuh believe mi? Here are some real-life examples of people who have paid the price for not filing taxes.

Case 1: Oswald's Seafood Restaurant

Mr. Oswald Powell was arrested and charged on Friday, January 27, 2017 for failure to comply with tax laws. He was granted a $30,000 bail under the condition that he would pay his outstanding tax returns for 2012 to 2015 by February 20, 2017 when he was scheduled to reappear in court.

Case 2: The Arrests of Christopher Reid and Renoree Graham

Christopher Reid and Renoree Graham were arrested in October 2015 for failure to file GCT, Income and Education taxes amounting to about $4 million. Their bail was set at

$200,000 and was only granted on the condition that they pay the outstanding taxes.

Case 3: 47 Chronically Delinquent Taxpayers Arrested in St. Ann

The Jamaica Gleaner reported on Tuesday, July 23, 2019 that 47 chronically delinquent taxpayers were arrested in a recent TAJ initiative to address a growing concern of tax avoidance. The TAJ plans to continue these "sweeps" and curb delinquency. The article did not clearly explain the type of taxes these people did not pay. However, it does highlight the fact that the TAJ is taking on a more active role in increasing tax compliance.

You do not want to be in the same boat as these tax delinquents. Get di ting right from start and just pay di taxes bredrin!

Setting Up Your TAJ Online Account

The business registration certificate that you receive from the Companies Office of Jamaica is only part of the business registration process. The next step is registering the business with the tax office so that you can get your business TRN. You should visit your local tax office to complete the process. They will ask you for your:

- Business registration certificate
- ID and TRN if you are setting up a sole proprietorship
- ID and TRN of all company directors if you are setting up a company

You will be asked to complete a form to set up your online account. Most taxes are now filed exclusively online so setting up this account is important. You can ask the representative to guide you through the process on a computer at the tax office. Speak with someone in the education department when you are done to ensure that your account is live, and you have been granted access to file the taxes relevant to your business.

Know the Tax Filing Forms

The type of taxes you file depends on the type of business you operate. It is important for you to know the relevant forms to complete, but it is also wise to get further guidance from either someone in the compliance department at your local tax office or a tax accountant. Here is a brief overview of some relevant forms.

Filing GCT

Remember that you don't need to file GCT if your sales revenue is less than $10 million. The form(s) that you would need to complete are:

- Form 4A- The General Consumption Tax Standard Return form is relevant to all registered taxpayers who provide goods and services outside of tourism activities and general insurance.

- Form 4C- The Special Consumption Tax Return form is relevant for businesses engaged in manufacturing and or importation of goods such as petroleum products, tobacco, spirits and beer.

- Form 4D- The General Consumption Tax Return for Tourism Activities form is relevant for businesses operating under the Tourist Board Act.

- Form 4E- The General Consumption Tax Return for General Insurance form is relevant for a business conducting general insurance activities. Insurance brokers and agents are also required to complete Schedule A of this form.

- Form 4G- This form is specifically for non-registered taxpayers who receive one-off payments, imported goods or services, or any other product or service that requires GCT payments.

Filing Self Employed Taxes

A self-employed person must complete 2 forms:

- SO4
- SO4a

The SO4a form is a declaration of your estimated income and the taxes that should be paid. It must be completed before the SO4 form. The SO4 form is used to capture information about your annual returns. It provides a true reflection of the money you have earned within the reporting period. You may be eligible for tax refunds or credits if the amount earned is less than the amount projected in your SO4a form. However, you will have to pay more if the amount earned is greater than the amount projected in your SO4a form.

There is one thing that online entrepreneurs tend to neglect- tax compliance. Even online businesses have to pay taxes and register with the Companies Office of Jamaica. There is a section of the SO4a form dedicated to declaring funds from overseas business endeavors. You cannot escape it. Register your business and ensure that it is tax compliant!

Additionally, you are required to file the following returns even if you are earning below the $1,509,600 threshold:

- Education tax

- NIS

- NHT

- Income tax

The ITO2 form is required for income tax filing. It must be accompanied by a balance sheet and income statement which a tax accountant can help you create.

Another important point to note is the fuzzy area that exists between running a side hustle while working for someone else full-time. The common thought is that it is not necessary to file taxes when earning money on the side because taxes are already taken out of your primary salary. The P24 form was created to dispel that myth. Any income you make outside of your full-time job is liable for twenty-five percent tax. Your employer should complete a P24 form and you should submit this form, along with your payment, before the March 15 deadline. The P24 form can only be accessed at your local tax office; it is not available online.

Filing Taxes for Employees

You are not required to file taxes for employees hired as independent contractors or freelancers. Independent contractors are typically hired on an as-needed basis and are responsible for filing their own taxes.

However, you are required to file taxes for employees hired either part-time or full-time to your company. You must file the education tax, NIS, NHT and income taxes for these employees. The SO1 Employer's Monthly Statutory Remittance Payroll form captures this information. The S02 Employer's Annual Return form provides an annual summary of the taxes filed for all employees.

When Should Taxes Be Filed?

A breakdown of when the forms previously mentioned should be filed is given in the table below.

Form	Date
Forms 4 a-g	GCT filings are due on or before the last working day of the month after the return period. For example, GCT for October is due on or before November 29.
SO4 and SO4a	There are 2 options: • Quarterly

	• Annually (before March 15)
ITO2	Before March 15
SO1	Monthly
SO2	Annually (before March 15)

These dates can change so keep abreast with news and updates on your TAJ portal. Also, ensure that you check the messages sent to you on your TAJ portal regularly so that you are aware of any potential issues that you need to address.

How Can You Keep Accurate Records?

Accurate record-keeping is crucial for filing taxes and getting external funding. Ask any accountant. An accountant's job is made ten times harder when the business does not keep track of income and expenses. Every receipt and invoice matters! Here are some tips to help you keep accurate records so that it is less likely that you will make mistakes during the tax filing process.

Identify Important Transactions

Accurate record-keeping is one of the most difficult elements of business, especially when you run a company that handles a large volume of daily transactions. Both entrepreneurs who run very small companies and those who run more elaborate enterprises need to keep accurate records.

Here are some transactions that you should keep track of if you are an entrepreneur working alone:

- Traveling expenses. How much do you spend on gas to travel to client meetings, conferences or other business-related events?
- What are your monthly utility costs?
- What is your weekly income?
- How much do you spend on monthly subscriptions relevant to the business?
- How much do you spend on your website subscription?
- How much do you spend on marketing monthly?

Knowing these numbers is one thing, having the invoices and receipts to support them is another. Keep a file where all your monthly bills, and the invoices you send to clients, are accurately filed. This will make it easier for you to create a monthly cash balance that helps you make informed decisions and paints an accurate picture of the taxes that you should file each quarter or each year.

Record-keeping becomes more intricate for entrepreneurs who operate businesses that handle a large amount of daily transactions. If you are one of these entrepreneurs, you need to get into what Greg Crabtree, author of "Simple Numbers, Straight Talk, Big Profits", calls a reporting rhythm. In fact, you may need to hire an employee whose sole responsibility is to provide you with these detailed reports.

An entrepreneur without a reporting rhythm is like a ship without a sail. Your numbers will get away from you, your ability to be proactive about potential challenges is greatly diminished and your ability to make informed financial decisions is hampered.

Crabtree provides useful information about the three categories of financial reporting (daily, weekly and monthly) that can help businesses get into an efficient reporting rhythm.

The Daily Cash Balance Report

You need to know how much money is in your account at the end of each business day. This report can easily be generated from accounting software such as QuickBooks. A low cash balance is cause for concern and may be an indication that you need to step in and fix a problem.

The Cash Flow Forecast Report

This report answers an important question, "Will you have enough money in the back when your bills are due?" It is based on a two-week projection of your expected sources of inflows and outflows. If you won't have enough money to pay your bills within the 2-week period, something needs to be done.

The Sales and Productivity Weekly Report

Crabtree discusses the importance of tracking your labor efficiency ratio to determine certain trends and deal with productivity issues. This ratio forms the basis of your sales and productivity weekly report. Feel free to read Crabtree's book to learn more. It really is a book for anyone who is serious about keeping abreast with their business' finances.

Digitize Your Documents

It is easy for data to get lost in piles of paperwork. Therefore, it is important now more than ever to create a seamless process to record your financial records digitally. We will discuss using accounting software in the next point, but I am presenting some applications (apps) here that you can use to transfer some of your hard copy financial records into a digital format.

- Expensify is the most popular receipt management app. You can capture receipts and produce mileage reports for trips taken on behalf of the company.
- Zoho Expense is another receipt tracking app that offers the same functionality as Expensify but at a faster speed.
- Mint Money Manager helps with budgeting and expense tracking.
- Goodbudget is a useful app for helping with preparing financial reports and analyzing expenditures.

It does not end here. The next step is organizing these scanned documents, analyzing the reports, and creating backup copies of all files. It will initially seem like a lot of work...too much for you to bear. However, the process will eventually become routine and less of a burden; it is the price you pay to get the results you need.

Use an Accounting App

QuickBooks is the accounting app that most people know. There are three types of subscriptions, each with an affordable monthly fee. All subscriptions allow you to:

- Track sales, expenses and profits
- Create and send unlimited customized invoices
- Track and manage sales tax
- Use the software with any mobile device

The Simple Start plan is a good plan for a small business owner who works alone and will only be sharing the software with an accountant. However, a larger organization that needs a report rhythm would benefit from the Plus plan.

Another app that has grown in popularity is Waves. It is not as sophisticated as QuickBooks, but it gets the job done and is free. You can use it to:

- Track income and expenses

- Send unlimited customized electronic invoices and receipts
- Scan receipts
- Carry out payroll if your local bank is supported
- Accept payments from customers if your local bank is supported

Waves and QuickBooks are the most common accounting apps. The one you choose depends on your budget and accounting needs. However, having an accounting app will help you keep accurate records and save you from major stress during tax filing season.

Hire an Accountant/ Bookkeeper

Bookkeepers record financial transactions while accountants interpret, classify, analyze, report and summarize financial data. Your business may need either a bookkeeper or an accountant or both.

Keeping track of finances can be overwhelming, especially for someone who is not good with numbers. It may seem possible initially to do everything on your own. In fact, an entrepreneur with a micro business that deals with small transactions may be better off doing everything for himself or herself. Hire an accountant or bookkeeper if you are doubtful about your ability to handle it all. It is better to have a professional keep your finances in check rather than make costly errors.

Key Points from Chapter Two

- Business registration makes your business legal and provides several benefits including increased funding opportunities, ease of banking and increased consumer confidence.

- Jamaican businesses are either registered under the Business Names Act or the Companies Act. The Super Form is used for registering both types of companies.

- It costs considerably less to register a sole proprietorship than to register a company. However, there is no clear separation between personal assets and business assets in a sole proprietorship.

- Owners of sole proprietorships are not required to file annual returns to the Companies Office. However, a sole proprietor should renew the business name every three years.

- Companies must file annual returns to the Companies Office. A non-profit company should complete Form 19b while a for-profit company should complete Form 19a.

- Remember to go to the tax office to register for your business TRN after you have received your business registration certificate from the Companies Office.

- GCT is only filed on revenue of $10 million or greater.

- Know the TAJ forms. There are forms for different purposes so it is important for you to know the forms that apply to your business and when they should be submitted along with the required payment.

- Keep accurate records.

- Digitize your documents so that it's easier to keep accurate financial records.

- Hire an accountant or bookkeeper to help you with keeping accurate financial records.

Checklist

- ☐ Complete and submit the Super Form.
- ☐ Pay relevant registration fee.
- ☐ Receive business registration certificate.
- ☐ Get relevant documents from the Department of Co-operatives and Friendly Societies if you are registering a non-profit company.
- ☐ Register business with the TAJ.
- ☐ Receive business TRN.

- ☐ Create online TAJ profile for ease of tax filing.

- ☐ Complete the relevant tax forms and submit them by the relevant due dates.

- ☐ Digitize invoices, receipts and other relevant business transactions.

- ☐ Use an accounting app to organize the digitized documents and conduct financial analyses.

- ☐ Hire a bookkeeper or accountant if necessary.

Reflection Question

What have you learnt about the business registration process?

_____

_____

_____

_____

_____

_____

_____

_____

_____

_____

_____

_____

_____

_____

_____

_____

_____

_____

_____

_____

Chapter Three: *Link Some Business Development Chargies*

The Government of Jamaica (GOJ) has created three powerful entities to support the MSME sector:

- The Jamaica Business Development Corporation (JBDC)
- The Development Bank of Jamaica (DBJ)
- The Export-Import (EXIM) Bank

Our leaders know that small businesses are the backbone of our economy. However, it may seem as though these organisations have been hidden in plain sight because few entrepreneurs are aware they exist. This chapter explains how each organisation can help you successfully start a business in Jamaica.

The JBDC

The JBDC was established in 2001 as an agency of the Ministry of Industry, Commerce, Agriculture and Fisheries. It functions through collaboration between public and private sector entities. The team works assiduously to provide business support services that help MSMEs thrive. There are offices in Kingston, Mandeville, Montego Bay and Westmoreland. The team offers services in five main areas:

- Technical services
- Business advisory services
- Marketing services
- Project management and research
- Financial support services

Technical Services

These services are offered through JBDC's Incubator Resource Centre which specializes in increasing the global competitiveness of businesses in the agro-processing, engineering, fashion and apparel, gift and craft, food services and communication industries. Some of the services offered include design counselling and product development.

Business Advisory Services

This team works with both established and novice entrepreneurs. The latter can benefit from validity assessments and customised training. The former can benefit from general consultations, operations audits and operations assessments.

Marketing Services

This team provides market access support through product market exposure, events marketing, linkage creation and trade show participation. Entrepreneurs can also receive training in marketing.

Project Management and Research

This team of research consultants provides research process outsourcing, market research, impact and needs assessment surveys, project management training, proposal writing and other related services.

Financial Support Services

This team of experts provides training, research, information about possible financing options and helps disburse grant funding to select MSMEs.

The DBJ

Founded in April 2000, the DBJ was established to create private sector development opportunities for all Jamaicans. The organization partners with a network of approved financial institutions (AFIs) to provide business loans for both large and small businesses. Additionally, they provide grants and business support services. There is a financing option for a business at any stage of the business life cycle. Visit their website at www.dbankjm.com to learn more about their services and how to apply for loans and grants

The EXIM Bank

The EXIM Bank is the oldest organization in this list. It was established in May 1986 and provides financing, insurance and business advisory services for businesses that depend heavily on exports and imports. One of the best features in the business advisory services section is connecting entrepreneurs with experienced business consultants. Visit their website at www.eximbankja.com for more details.

Key Points from Chapter Three

- There are three government agencies that provide the business advisory and financial support your business needs.

- The JBDC is the best place to go for business advice regardless of the stage at which you are at in your business.

- The DBJ is the best place to go for grants and attractive business loans.

- The EXIM Bank is useful for businesses that depend heavily on export and import.

Checklist

- ☐ Get business advice from the JBDC.
- ☐ Research the requirements to apply for a loan or grant at the DBJ and the EXIM Bank.

Reflection Questions

Which of the three agencies mentioned can best assist you with starting your business? What do you need to do to benefit from what this agency offers?

_____

_____

_____

_____

_____

_____

_____

_____

_____

_____

_____

_____

_____

_____

_____

_____

_____

Chapter Four: *Money Will Wash Weh*

Do you remember the days when Macka Diamond's catch phrase "Money O!" was the hottest dancehall trend. It painted a picture of money raining down from the skies to facilitate a lavish lifestyle. Wannabe entrepreneurs tend to have a "Money O!" mentality. They expect that their business will earn a continuous stream of income that can help them get rich quick. That is not how it works in real life. Consider the fable of a boy and some filberts (more commonly known as hazelnuts).

The Boy and the Filberts
Extracted from the book "Aesop for Children"

A Boy was given permission to put his hand into a pitcher to get some filberts. But he took such a great fistful that he could not draw his hand out again. There he stood, unwilling to give up a single filbert and yet unable to get them all out at once. Vexed and disappointed he began to cry.

"My boy," said his mother, *"be satisfied with half the nuts you have taken and you will easily get your hand out. Then perhaps you may have some more filberts some other time."*

The Lesson

Greed comes before a downfall. Your business' income is not there for you to take fistfuls for personal gain.

You know that money is crucial for getting your business off the ground, but startup financing is often difficult to find. Wise entrepreneurs understand the four business funding options, when to apply them and how to choose the right investments that improve the business' cash flow. However, this does not mean that you will not make mistakes. Even the wisest entrepreneurs have had some hiccups as they try to fund business growth and adequately manage finances.

There are four main business funding options:
- Bootstrapping
- Debt
- Investors (Equity)
- Grants

Funding Option #1: Bootstrapping

Bootstrapping is the process of using your own finances, and the business' first sales, to fund business growth. It can be one of the most difficult, but most rewarding, ways to finance a business. A lot of planning and preparation is necessary to successfully start a business using personal finances. The process begins at least a year or two before you leave your full-time job since your full time job is your primary source of income and what you have already probably been using to finance certain elements of the business.

The financial transition from leaving your full-time job to focus on your business involves 3 core principles. Understand that it will not be easy; it will require tremendous sacrifice. However, following these three core principles will save you a lot of stress and struggle in the short term.

The Three Core Principles of the Financial Transition from the 9 to 5

Principle #1

Bills will always be there. How do you plan to pay them? I suggest that you save enough money to cover your expenses for at least the first 3 months after you make the transition.

Look at your monthly budget and identify the recurring expenses that you cannot avoid such as your car loan payments, rent, groceries, and utility bills.

Not saving enough means that you will be depending solely on the business to finance your basic needs. Risk-takers live for this and there is nothing wrong with being a risk-taker and diving in headfirst. However, be practical especially if you have a family to take care of. Start saving to cover these expenses at least a year before you plan to leave your 9 to 5.

Principle #2

Create rainy day investments. Investing is different from saving. Keeping your money in a savings account guarantees little to no returns. However, investing in real estate, stocks, bonds and other forms of equity present opportunities for greater returns. An investment account is important as a back-up plan for those months when your business is taking a while to gain traction and you have bills to pay.

Although investing a large sum of money can help you gain more returns, it is possible to start investing with as little as $10,000. The point is to be consistent by investing the same amount (or more) of money each month until you have created a nice nest egg. This nest egg is something that you will need to fall back on to either finance a business or personal emergency.

Principle #3

Do not leave too soon. You may be itching to leave your job. It makes you feel unfulfilled and burnt out and consumes time that you should be using to build your business. Take a deep breath because you do not want to make any rash decisions. There is never really a perfect time to leave your full-time job. However, setting the stage for a somewhat smooth transition by ensuring that your finances are in order helps immensely.

How to Bootstrap Without Burning Through Your Personal Finances

Depending solely on personal finances to fund your business is risky. All startups experience what is called a burn rate which is the rate at which the company is losing money. It is usually quoted as a monthly rate. For instance, a burn rate of 100,000 JMD per month means that the company is losing 100,000 JMD per month.

Businesses consume a lot of capital, especially in the beginning phases. It is wise to grow your business to a point where your burn rate is either considerably low or non-existent before you leave a stable source of income. Nevertheless, you may be at a crossroads where you have no choice but to leave your stable income to make your business something profitable. Here are some tips to help you reduce your burn rate and the risk of spending all your personal finances:

- Put every cent you earn back into the business from its inception straight to the end of the 3-month period after you have left your 9 to 5. This is the time for you to work extra hard to ensure that the business is earning enough to support paying you a salary.

- Use freelancers and independent contractors as much as possible instead of hiring full-time staff. Freelancers and independent contractors can produce high-quality work for a fraction of the cost of a full-time employee.

- Do not rent a storefront unless it is absolutely necessary. Work from home as much as possible. A coworking space is also an option.

- Do not live above your means. Your lifestyle may be too expensive for you to maintain at this stage. Get rid of unnecessary expenses.

- Do not take on more than what your business needs at each phase of development. There are often creative solutions to some of the problems you face; you just need to spend the time doing research.

- Create a business account so that there is a clear separation between your personal finances and your business' revenue. You will need your:
    - o Business registration certificate
    - o Proof of address
    - o Two forms of identification

I have found that Jamaica Money Market Brokers (JMMB) offers the best business account for a micro business owner because I was only required to have 1,000 JMD to start the account. However, that may just be a matter of preference. The bank you choose depends on your preferences, the size of your business, and the amount of money you have to put down an initial deposit.

Funding Option #2: Debt

Your business may be growing at a rate where bootstrapping is no longer feasible. Therefore, you may need to borrow some money to purchase the necessary equipment and competencies to facilitate growth. Thankfully, the Private Sector Organization of Jamaica recently launched an initiative to make it easier for MSMEs to access funding. It is called the Access to Finance Facilitation Panel for SMEs and was launched in July 2019.

There have been constant complaints from MSMEs about the difficulty they often face when trying to get business loans. Jamaica's leading financial institutions have heard the cries and created this initiative to work with the MSME Alliance, and other key stakeholders, to find the best solutions for startup financing so that Jamaica's MSME industry can grow.

One solution that has been brought forward is the use of moveable-assets as loan collateral. Therefore, an MSME could apply for a loan using assets such as accounts receivable, inventory and equipment. This suggestion has not yet been introduced but it is at least a step in the right direction.

Nevertheless, debt should be a last resort for a growing business. Although it can help reduce the amount paid in taxes annually, it is a heavy financial obligation that can suck the business dry if high revenue generating investments are not acquired with the debt. Therefore, you must be very strategic about when you want to apply for a business loan. Take out a loan too soon and your business will be dead before it even really begins.

Funding Option #3: Investors/ Equity

Another investment option is to give up equity in your business in exchange for investment. You will hear some entrepreneurs talking about trying to maintain equity so that they have enough for different investment rounds. This type of funding shows that there are external stakeholders who believe in your business' potential, but it also threatens your ownership rights to the company.

Give up too much equity and you may no longer be a majority shareholder. Other shareholders may come together to form a voting block and organize a company takeover or vote against resolutions presented at shareholder meetings. The money is great but the long-term effect of having these people or entities as a part of your business can be detrimental.

On the other hand, it is possible to find the right investors who add value to the business. The trick is knowing where to find these investors and understanding how much equity you should give up. Here are some tips to help with your decision:

- Sign up for the Angel Investment Network by visiting www.caribbeaninvestmentnetwork.com/jamaican-investors. Here is how to effectively use the platform:
  - o Identify a list of 50 investors on the website to whom you would like to pitch your business.
  - o Send in a request for your pitch to be sent to these investors.
  - o Publish your pitch on the platform so that anyone can see it.
  - o Respond to messages from interested investors.

- Send a pitch to the FirstAnglesJa team. Visit this website to learn how you can do this www.firstangelsjamaica.proseeder.com

- Attend networking events and make connections. We will discuss this further in an upcoming chapter.

- Ask family and friends.

How to Create a Winning Investor Pitch

An investor pitch is a quick way to let potential investors know about your business. Investors generally do not have a lot of time to read through voluminous business plans or sit through lengthy presentations. Therefore, your investor pitch should be quick and engaging. An investor pitch can be an elevator pitch or a full-length pitch. Each pitch has unique characteristics that are worth discussing.

The Elevator Pitch

Have you ever been in an elevator? The time it takes to travel from one floor to the next is often less than a minute. Picture running into an elevator and seeing Don Wehby, Chief Executive Officer of Grace Kennedy Limited. He turns to you and says, "I have heard good things about you. Tell me about your business." That elevator ride could make or break your chances of winning him as an investor. Therefore, you have to be as compelling as possible in that one-minute period before the elevator ride ends.

This analogy perfectly sums up an elevator pitch. Critical investment for your business depends on how well you use that one-minute timeframe. A good elevator pitch should have a hook, a value proposition and a call to action.

- **The Hook:** The hook is based on what makes your business interesting. You are introducing yourself and describing the problem that your business is solving in a unique way. Add a bit of wit and humor and you are setting the stage for a good elevator ride. The hook should ideally be no more than a sentence.

- **The Value Proposition:** The value proposition follows. It is the meat of your pitch. This is where you explain the immense value your business provides using a real-life example. Your aim is to show the benefits of your product or service and the fact that customers are already using it and are pleased with the results. Try not to make this portion be longer than 2 sentences.

- **The Call to Action:** The call to action is the cherry on top. Ask for an appropriate response to this short interaction. The response could be a follow-up call, meeting, appointment or simply exchanging business cards. The interaction should always end with an appropriate call-to-action.

The Full-Length Pitch

A full-length pitch is usually a 10-minute presentation in front of a single investor or a panel of investors. You will need a pitch deck for this presentation. A pitch deck is an electronic presentation, created using presentation software such as PowerPoint or Prezi, which provides a quick overview of your business. It can be considered a synopsis of your business plan. Here are some tips for creating a good pitch deck:

- The first two slides should summarize the key elements of your business in a visually appealing way. These slides function like the executive summary of your business plan.

- Describe what makes your product or service unique, how it benefits the customer, and testimonials from actual users of the product or service. This should not take up more than three or four slides.

- Describe your marketing strategy in one or two slides. How do you plan to find and retain customers?

- Describe your management team and the value they bring in no more than two slides.

- Include well summarized financial projections and current financial information in no more than two slides.

- Ensure that the presentation is engaging and fit for your audience.

Funding Option #4: Grants

Grants are non-repayable funds given by one party to another. The DBJ and JBDC are good places to get assistance with finding grants appropriate for your business. The JBDC will help you develop the skills to write winning grant proposals. The DBJ offers the following types of financial assistance:

- Special loans
- Grants
- Venture capital

You may think that it is strange for organizations and individuals to give away money without expecting anything in return; all they really want is to see the money being used for its intended purpose. Organizations tend to give grants away because they see a need in the community that they want to fill. In fact, there are several grants offered for the development of businesses in developing countries like Jamaica. However, most of these grants tend to be offered to non-profit organizations.

Here is a list of some places where you can apply for grant funding:

- Jamaica Social Investment Fund
- Digicel Jamaica Foundation
- JN Foundation
- The American Friends of Jamaica
- DBJ
- Environmental Health Foundation

How to Write a Strong Grant Proposal

The JBDC has a team of experts that can help you write a strong grant proposal but here are some tips to help you start the process.

- Read the Funding Opportunity Announcement (FOA) carefully. Each grant has different application requirements. Pay attention to these and ensure that you check all the boxes.

- Consult with your team to determine if the organization is at a stage where it can commit to the grant project. There will be some stipulations about how the funds can be spent and the conditions under which you will be able to access the funds.

Most grant proposals have nine parts:
- o Cover letter
- o Executive summary
- o Need statement
- o Goals and objectives
- o Methods, strategies or program design
- o Evaluation
- o Other funding or sustainability
- o Information about your organization

o   Project budget

- Do some research to determine what should be included in each of these sections. You may need a skilled writer to consult with your team, ensure that the content is engaging and adequately convey your message.

- Focus on what you are going to do to address the problem or need rather than the problems your organization faces.

- The budget should match up with the picture you have been painting throughout the proposal.

Key Points from Chapter 4

- Be wise about how you spend the money your business earns. It is not meant for instant gratification.

- There are four ways to fund your business: bootstrapping, debt, investment or grants.

- Debt should be the funding source of last resort.

- Always have an elevator pitch prepared in your head. You never know when you will get an opportunity to pitch to an investor.

Checklist

- ☐ Prepare a budget for your business' current expenses.

- ☐ Determine how you can use personal funds to finance these expenses until the business can fund itself.

- ☐ Determine if your business is at a point where additional funding is necessary.

- ☐ Search for investors or affordable loans.

- ☐ Create a business bank account.

- ☐ Get help from the JBDC to write your grant proposal if you own a non-profit.

Reflection Questions

What is the best funding option for the stage at which your business is presently? What do you need to do to make that funding option work?

_____

_____

_____

_____

_____

_____

_____

_____

_____

_____

_____

_____

_____

_____

_____

_____

Chapter Five: *Links Run Tings*

The concept of "links run tings" has dominated the Jamaican landscape for decades. High colored men and women were almost guaranteed to advance in the status quo because of the color of their skin. The tides have shifted a bit. Sure, these men and women tend to be treated better than the average Joe when doing business. However, it is now more about who you know and the connections that you can create regardless of your complexion.

You may be thinking, "How am I going to meet prominent Jamaican figures like Joseph Matalon, Gordon Stewart or William Mahfood? They are the only people who can really get me the links I need to create a successful business." Of course, it helps to know people in high places, but it is impossible for all 2.89 million people in Jamaica to have links in all the right places. This does not mean that all 2.89 million people cannot find other valuable links that make business success possible. It is time to change your thinking because trying to find the *right* links will prevent you from creating valuable connections with seemingly ordinary people.

Let me share a fable with you that highlights the importance of not discrediting the links that you can make with seemingly ordinary people.

Aesop's Fable of the Lion and the Mouse
Extracted from the book "Aesop for Children"

A Lion lay asleep in the forest, his great head resting on his paws. A timid little Mouse came upon him unexpectedly, and in her fright and haste to get away, ran across the Lion's nose. Roused from his nap, the Lion laid his huge paw angrily on the tiny creature to kill her.

"Spare me!" begged the poor Mouse. "Please let me go and someday I will surely repay you."

The Lion was much amused to think that a Mouse could ever help him. But he was generous and finally let the Mouse go.

Some days later, while stalking his prey in the forest, the Lion was caught in the toils of a hunter's net. Unable to free himself, he filled the forest with his angry roaring. The Mouse knew the voice and quickly found the Lion struggling in the net. Running to one of the great ropes that bound him, she gnawed it until it parted, and soon the Lion was free.

"You laughed when I said I would repay you," said the Mouse. "Now you see that even a Mouse can help a Lion."

The Lessons
- Be kind and gracious to those you meet.
- Someone who you think cannot help you today may just be the person who helps you tomorrow.
- Value all the connections you make.

Getting "links" is all about putting yourself out there and being a part of networking opportunities. I have found that I have made some lasting connections through Success Lifestyle Magazine that have helped me learn so much more about the business world and gain new clients.

There are two main ways to get meaningful links: create your own networking opportunities or attend networking events.

Part One: Create Networking Opportunities

Each day provides a networking opportunity. Networking, at its core, is all about meeting new people and creating new experiences. It often requires stepping out of our comfort zones, especially if meeting new people is not something you like doing. Let me be brutally honest; creating networking opportunities is something that I have struggled with because I am a strong introvert. However, I have grown to realize that it may be challenging but it is not impossible. You never know who the next person you meet will become someday.

Read that last sentence again. It is one of the most powerful lessons I have learnt as I have gotten older. Some of my high school and university batch mates are now in prominent positions in Jamaica. Let me give you some examples. One of my UWI batchmates, who I lived with on Rex Nettleford Hall, is a highly sought-after top executive for a prominent international brand. Another of my hallmates is a regional marketing manager. One of my high school and university batch mates is making waves as a poignant young Jamaican political leader. *You never know who the next person you meet will become someday.*

I worked with the batchmates I mentioned on various projects throughout my university years and we built a good working relationship. Therefore, I know that I can contact them at any time to present feasible business propositions. They may not always be in a position to assist with what I am presenting, but they are at least willing to help out if they can.

Do not take the people you meet now for granted. The most unassuming person can become someone great and even inspire you to become your best self. Here are some ways that you can create opportunities to meet new people daily. These pointers may seem more applicable to introverts but there may just be something in there that extroverts can learn from.

Interact with Your Coworkers

There is an unspoken rule in some workplaces that your coworkers cannot be your friends. The reality is that there is at least one person at work who you can call your friend because this person makes being at work bearable. Having this work friend is great. However, you should interact with more of your coworkers.

I became more confident about interacting with my coworkers about three years into my last job. I attended all staff functions, engaged in activities and even spearheaded the creation of a Staff Welfare Committee. I took the time to get to know most of my coworkers and developed a good rapport with them. Here are some additional strategies that can help increase your interaction with your coworkers:

- Start positive lunchtime conversations in the lunchroom.

- Leave a word of encouragement on a coworker's desk.

- Volunteer to work on projects with other teams within the organization.

- Be proactive about addressing issues that your coworkers face within the workplace that are within your control.

You may have gotten to a point where you do not want to interact with any of your coworkers because of how toxic they seem. Separate the behavior from the person and make a conscious effort to respond differently. If you make a greater effort to shine a positive light despite the darkness that surrounds you, you will find that the light becomes contagious and you will see your coworkers in a different light.

Connect with People on Social Media

Rochele Spencer, the well-known founder and fashion designer from Yours Truly Rochele, taught me an important lesson when I interviewed her for Success Lifestyle Magazine's fourth issue. She mentioned that fellow local fashion designer Rhea Imani is one of her greatest sources of inspiration. Most people would have viewed a competitor as a threat and would have done anything in their power to downplay what their competitor has done.

Not Rochele. She started following Rhea Imani on Instagram and they ended up having a conversation with each other via Instagram messaging. A competitor had now become a friend. They support each other's businesses unreservedly. Rochele passes on any designs that she believes better fit Rhea's aesthetic and vice versa. Rhea inspired Rochele to create her own showroom. You get the idea. Even your competitors can become your greatest allies.

I have even personally experienced the power of social media as a networking tool. I ran a Giveaway Bonanza contest in January 2019 to increase the exposure of Success Lifestyle Magazine's Instagram page. The third-place winner, Sara-Lou Morgan-Walker, tugged at my heart strings. She runs a non-profit organization called the Angelic Ladies Society that addresses some important concerns for at-risk girls. Instead of using her Fontana gift voucher to buy things for herself, she used it to purchase items for a vision board activity she was planning with the girls.

I knew that I had to feature her in one of the magazine's issues. Her story resonated with me and I knew that it could inspire others. Therefore, I featured her in the one-year anniversary issue (issue five) of the magazine. We now have a good work relationship.

Social media is a great way to meet new people. Here are a few ways that you can use social media to network:

- Respond to comments made on your posts to encourage greater discussion and learn more about your customers. The more you learn, the more likely it is that you will be able to notice a mutually beneficial connection.

- Join relevant LinkedIn groups and actively engage in discussions. Do not view these groups solely as a means to promote your products, services or online content.

- Participate in Twitter chats.

- Join Facebook groups and participate in the discussions. Use these groups to get advice and make the most of opportunities to express genuine interest in what other people in the group are doing.

- Use Instagram hashtags to find profiles. Follow the profiles that interest you and engage with the content on these profiles.

- Use Follwerwonk to find and connect with influencers on Twitter in your niche.

Volunteer

Pearl S. Buck once said, "To serve is beautiful but only if it is done with joy, a whole heart, and a free mind." Volunteering is a good way to meet new people and establish strong connections. However, it should not be done if that is your sole objective. It is something that you should do willingly because you want to positively impact other people's lives.

Here are some ways that you can volunteer:

- Become actively involved in the charity division of your full-time job. For instance, the Joan Duncan Foundation is the charity division of the JMMB Group. A JMMB employee can find out the activities in which the Foundation engages and volunteer to be a part of them.

- You may work in a company that does not do much charity work. Why not start charity projects for the company? Charity projects are a good way for a company to meet its corporate social responsibility obligations. There are a good investment in the long-term.

- Join charity organizations such as the Rotaract Club or the Kiwanis Club.

- Give some of your time to the programs at your local community centre.

- Work on some projects for free. You will feel the financial pinch initially, but people will recommend you if you produce high-quality work.

- Be bold enough to step outside of Jamaica's borders and join an international charity organization. Here are a few possibilities:
    o UNICEF
    o The Salvation Army
    o The Red Cross
    o Habitat for Humanity
    o International Volunteers Association
    o Volunteer Abroad
    o UN Volunteers

- Teach a class at your local community centre or church.
- Sign Up for a Work and Travel Program

Travel

There are 195 countries in the world. Sure, no weh nuh betta dan yaad but you can learn so much and meet new people if you sign up for a work and travel program. Travelling also broadens your perspective and can help you:

- Find new business ideas
- Meet people who can help your business reach an international customer base
- Incorporate elements of foreign cultures into the Jamaican experience

You don't have to make preparations to legally stay in the new country indefinitely. Instead, you can stay for a year or for the length of time stipulated in the contract then come right back home and start developing your business.

The United States, Canada and the United Kingdom are ***not*** the only options for a work and travel program. We tend to limit ourselves to these countries because many members of the Jamaican diaspora live there. There are work and travel opportunities in the Middle East, Asia, and even Australia.

Teaching English as a second language is one of the most common ways to get work and travel opportunities. It helps to either have a first degree in English or the Teach English as a Foreign Language (TEFL) certification. You can find these opportunities at:

- TEFL.org https://www.tefl.org/en/
- The Japan Teaching and Exchange Program http://jetprogramme.org/en/
- International Schools around the World https://www.teachaway.com/international-schools

Here are some other work and travel opportunities that are not based on teaching English.

Option #1: Overseas Work and Travel
Website: https://overseasworkandtravel.com/
Who is it for? College and university students who want a summer job.

Option #2: International Recruiting Staffing Solutions Inc.
Website: https://irssworktravel.com/

Who is it for? Those seeking short-term work in the hospitality industry

Option #3: JOYST Youth Exchange International Ltd.
Website: https://www.joystyouthexchangeintl.org/
Who is it for? Students and other youth

Option #4: F.A.R.M.S
Website: http://farmsontario.ca/
Who is this for? Adults looking for seasonal agricultural work

Part Two: Attend Business Networking Events

Business networking events are specifically created to help entrepreneurs and other business professionals meet and form business relationships. Some of the best places to find business events in Jamaica include:

- Eventbrite
- Business Events Ja
- Jamaica Business Development Corporation (JBDC)
- The social media pages of most major Jamaican banks. For instance, JMMB hosts events throughout the year that can provide networking opportunities.

- CoWork Ja's Instagram page
- Nexxub's Instagram page
- Small Business Association of Jamaica
- Young Entrepreneurs Association of Jamaica

How to Benefit from a Business Networking Experience

Business networking can be a rewarding experience if you understand how to make the most of the opportunity. Here are some things that you should do to truly benefit from a business networking experience:

- Be prepared to listen to others and express genuine interest in their businesses and ideas. It is easy to enter a business networking experience thinking that you should only focus on promoting your business. Your elevator pitch game deh pan point so yuh a try use it up. People nah pay yuh no mind if yuh nuh show interest in wah dem a seh. Real talk.

- Try to establish mutually beneficial relationships. How can you help another entrepreneur solve a problem in his business?

- Always carry your business cards. It makes it easier to exchange contact information. Despite what some people say, business cards have not gone out of style.

- Do not be afraid to make the first move.

- Remember that follow-up is important. You went to the business networking event to make connections. How pointless would it be to make connections at the event but forget about them after?

Key Points from Chapter 5

- You do not have to know the most prominent people in Jamaica in order to get ahead. Knowing them helps but it does not mean that your success is thwarted if you do not.

- Begin each day with the mindset that you have been provided with a chance to create a networking opportunity.

- Do not be afraid to travel. Experiencing new cultures and meeting people outside of Jamaica can help you create strong connections to expand your business endeavors.

- Business networking opportunities exist in Jamaica. Do you know how to benefit from them?

Checklist

- ☐ Identify 2 ways that you can create networking opportunities and implement them.
- ☐ Create business cards.
- ☐ Attend at least one business networking event per quarter.

Reflection Question

What steps will you take to engage in networking activities this month?

_____

_____

_____

_____

_____

_____

_____

_____

_____

_____

_____

_____

_____

_____

_____

_____

_____

_____

Chapter Six: *Di Marketing Ting Haffi Tun Up*

A great business idea is nothing without a solid marketing plan; marketing is what sells your business. The following elements are essential for a good marketing strategy:

- A clear understanding of the target audience
- A variety of advertising media to attract varying interests
- Consistency
- Regular evaluation so that best practices can be noted, or adjustments made as necessary
- Segmentation and personalization

5 Steps for Creating a Good Marketing Strategy

Step 1: Set clear goals.

There must be a way to measure whether each marketing campaign has been successful. Your marketing strategy will be multifaceted and include social media marketing (SMM), content marketing, digital marketing, and traditional advertising. Therefore, there will be a variety of campaigns running concurrently. ***Each campaign must have a SMARTER goal.***

SMARTER is an acronym that stands for:

S- Specific

It is important to be specific about what you want to achieve with each campaign. For instance, saying that you are running a social media campaign to get more followers is not enough. Instead, you could say "We will run a 20 percent discount offer on our women's shoes to get more followers on our Facebook page."

M- Measurable

The goal should be quantifiable. How will you know if the campaign has been successful if there is no way to measure this success? Let us go back to the social media campaign example. "Get more followers" is still too vague. You can make the objective measurable by saying, "We will run a 20 percent discount offer on our women's shoes to get 20 new followers on our Facebook page." Therefore, the campaign will only be successful if you have gained 20 or more followers.

A- Attainable

Do not set a goal that would be impossible for you to achieve. For instance, if the current trend on your Facebook page is to get 2 new followers per month with your regular posts, you cannot expect to see a drastic jump to 20 new followers. As a result, you may need to modify the goal to say, "We will run a 20 percent discount offer on our women's shoes to get 10 new followers on our Facebook page."

R- Relevant

Your marketing campaigns should be relevant to both your business and your target audience. For instance, the 20 percent discount offer on women's shoes would be irrelevant to your male customers. A different campaign is needed for each market segment.

T- Time bound

The marketing campaigns will not last forever. There must be a cut-off point. We can make the goal used in our discount example time-bound by saying, "We will run a 20 percent discount offer on our women's shoes from March 25 to 30 to get 10 new followers on our Facebook page by the end of the month."

E- Evaluated

Evaluating a marketing campaign is more than looking at it at the end to determine if the measurable element has been achieved. Evaluation is an ongoing process that should be done throughout the campaign. You should plan the intervals at which you are going to evaluate the campaign's progress. Let us go back to the discount example.

The campaign will last for 5 days (March 25 to 30). You are using A/B testing to determine which type of ad attracts more of your target audience. Test A has a traditional discount poster while test B has a promotional video. You should plan to track the results of each campaign daily to determine which produces the better results so that you maximise your return on investment (ROI) for the marketing campaign.

R- Reviewed

Revision is often necessary after evaluating a marketing campaign. Let us say that you realize that test B was costing less per click than test A after two days. You could choose to discard test A or modify it so that you can get better results.

Step 2: Create buyer personas.

Goal setting creates the foundation for the marketing campaign. However, that step becomes more meaningful when you clearly understand your target audience. Buyer personas help create this understanding. HubSpot defines a buyer persona as "a semi-fictional representation of your ideal customer based on market research and real data about your existing customers."

Buyer personas help with personalization and segmentation. Customers now expect companies to provide an experience that specifically caters to their individual needs.

Treating all of them the same will not work. Your marketing campaigns must, therefore, be personalized and divided into the various customer segments that your business serves.

A buyer persona has:

- An avatar or picture that represents the customer being described. It helps to have this visual representation of the customer to make it seem more real.
- A fictional name of the customer. You will use this name while planning your marketing campaigns.
- The customer's demographics: location, age, gender, marital status, occupation, annual income and education level.
- The customer's interests and hobbies.
- The customer's pain point.

Here is an example of a buyer persona for our discount campaign.

Name: Jane

Age: 28

Gender: Female

Occupation: Teacher

Location: Mandeville

Income: 1,800,000 JMD per annum

Children: 2

Marital status: Single

Interests: Keeping up with the latest fashion trends

Pain Point: Jane wants to look stylish without spending too much money. She tends to shop at Payless and always looks for the best deals. However, the shoes she gets there are common; she wants her shoes to be bold and different.

Your campaign is now "The Jane Campaign" and will be created to suit the needs of customers who are similar to her.

Step 3: Create a content marketing plan.

As stated earlier, a marketing strategy is multi-faceted; there will be several campaigns running concurrently. These campaigns work together to take a potential customer through the sales funnel so that he or she moves from interested customer to paying customer. A content marketing plan helps bring all these campaigns together and has the following elements:

- A theme for each quarter with sub-themes for each month.

- An overarching objective for the quarter that is broken down into smaller monthly objectives.

- An outline of the content that will be created, published and distributed on a daily and weekly basis. Content can include blog articles, videos, podcasts, social media posts, infographics and many other options.

- An indication of who will produce each content piece and when it will be published.

- A call-to-action for each piece that will result in the attainment of the goals for both the quarter and the month.

Here is an example of a content marketing plan for Janny's Accessories, a company that sells women's shoes, clothing, handbags, and jewelry. This example only contains the plan for the first month in the quarter. A detailed plan would have an outline for all 3 months.

2019 Quarter One Content Marketing Plan
Janny's Accessories
January-March 2019

Theme: Mix and match pieces can make a statement.
Goal: To acquire at least ten recurring customers through the online platform by March 31.

Month: January
Theme: Change your wardrobe for the new year so that you always walk into work with a bang.
Goal: Have at least five customers sign-up for our corporate makeover service.
N.B.- All content pieces should have a call-to-action

January 1: Happy New Year Corporate Chic Infographic for IG and FB pages
**Hire an infographic designer and schedule it for posting.

January 3: Post a blog article about trending colors in corporate wear in 2019. Hire a content writer who understands Search Engine Optimisation (SEO).

January 5: Launch social media ad campaign featuring a 1-minute video about the benefits of looking good at work. Hire a videographer, social media marketer, models and makeup artist. Do the shoot in mid-December and have the video ready for posting by January 3

January 7: Post a wardrobe Tip of The Week on Instagram (IG) and Facebook (FB). Use Canva to create the graphic.

January 10: Post a blog article about how to find a good clothing store for corporate wear in Jamaica. Hire a content writer who understands SEO

January 12: Paid social media advertising campaign ends.

January 14: Post a wardrobe Tip of the Week on IG and FB. Use Canva to create the graphic.

January 17 Post a blog article about finding the right shoes for corporate wear. Hire a content writer who understands SEO.

January 21: Post a wardrobe Tip of the Week on IG and FB. Use Canva to create the graphic.

January 24: Post a blog article about how to get business fashion inspiration from Jamaica's leading fashionistas. Hire a content writer who understands SEO.

January 25: Launch the Wardrobe Mania podcast that features fashion experts who teach listeners how to take their wardrobes from drab to fab. Buy the necessary equipment to create the podcast in January. Send out teasers each week to email subscribers and social media followers. Have guests scheduled by the end of December.

January 28: Post a wardrobe Tip of the Week on IG and FB. Use Canva to create the graphic.

January 31 Post a blog article about pairing the right accessories with corporate wear. Hire a content writer who understands SEO.

Does this seem overwhelming? Let the Success Lifestyle Magazine team help you create a comprehensive content marketing plan. We can also help you find freelance professionals who can bring all elements of the plan to life. Contact us at info@successlifestylemagazine.com for more information.

Step 4: Learn from your competitors.

Your competitors teach some of the best lessons. It is important for you to learn from their mistakes so that you do not repeat them in your own marketing campaigns. Look at the type of content that your competitors post on their social media pages. Pay attention to their print, television and billboard campaigns. Here are some questions that you should answer in your analysis:

- What do customers like about their content?
- What makes their content unique?
- What can I do differently to showcase the uniqueness of my brand?
- How can I adjust my marketing efforts so that I do not make the same mistakes as this brand?

Step 5: Set a budget and execute.

The previous steps were only about planning. However, a plan is meaningless if it is not implemented. This is the stage where you set your budget and execute the respective marketing campaigns for each segment of your customer base.

Setting a marketing budget can be tricky, especially if you are a small business owner who has little money. This budget is necessary though if you want to run successful marketing campaigns. Here are some factors to consider when setting your marketing budget:

- Allocate about eight percent of your revenue to advertising.

- Ensure that you know how you are going to achieve your marketing goals at each stage of your business' growth. This will help you gauge the amount of money needed for marketing at each stage.

- Budget for recurring marketing expenses such as email marketing software, Content Resource Management (CRM) software and website hosting.

- Remember that your budget should be flexible to accommodate changes to your marketing plan.

- Keep abreast with marketing trends so that you know how to adjust your budget and stay ahead of the competition.

- Spend wisely by keeping tabs on how your marketing campaigns are performing. End poor performing campaigns before they consume your budget.

Why should you create a website?

Jamaican businesses have been slow in catching on to the value of a business website. Those who do not have a website are missing out on the benefits of digital marketing. Your website acts as the focal point for the seamless integration of all your digital marketing efforts.

Digital marketing has several branches including:

- Content marketing
- Social media marketing
- Search Engine Optimization (SEO)
- Email marketing

Content Marketing and SEO

Content marketing and SEO are closely related. SEO focuses on the use of keywords, keyword phrases, backlinks, meta titles and meta descriptions. This may seem like a lot for a person without a marketing background but doing some basic research about SEO and all it entails can help you make the best use of your website. Your business' website is your brand's online real estate and it helps you leverage the power of content marketing and SEO. Essentially, these 2 elements of digital marketing increase your brand's visibility and, therefore, your ability to win new customers.

Each page on your website offers an SEO opportunity. It begins with keyword research so that you can identify the keywords and keyword phrases that relate to your business' niche. Search engines are putting less emphasis on keywords now, but they are still important to help with search engine ranking. The keywords and keyword phrases that you have identified should be included in each page's:

- Headings (H1, H2, H3)

- Content

- Meta tags (description of the page's content that displays in search engine results)

The next step is to create a blog which is one of the best ways to establish your brand as an industry expert and attract potential customers through value-added content. High quality articles are consistently posted on a well-developed blog and these articles attempt to:

- Answer customers' burning questions

- Give Do IT Yourself (DIY) tips

- Provide your unique perspective on industry-related issues

- Showcase case studies of customers who have used your product or service and achieved amazing results

Your website's blog should have the SEO basics which include:

- Keywords in the content and H1, H2 and H3 headings

- Keywords in each blog post's meta description

- Internal and external links. Internal links connect that post to other pages on your website. External links connect that post to other websites that support your claims or add value to what is being discussed in the article.

- Backlinks which are links on external websites that direct people to your website. These links are often difficult to create.

However, content marketing does not end with blog posts. It really includes any type of content that you post online. Therefore, it includes YouTube videos, podcasts, infographics, eBooks and a wide range of digital content. Does this all seem overwhelming to you? We have not even touched local SEO and SEO for voice search! Take a deep breath and contact the Success Lifestyle Magazine team at info@successlifestylemagazine.com. We have a team of content marketing experts who understand how to use content marketing to give your brand the exposure that it needs.

Social Media Marketing (SMM)

SMM is the form of digital marketing with which most Jamaicans are familiar. We are quick to create Instagram profiles, Facebook business pages, Twitter accounts, Pinterest accounts...whatever social media platform we think we understand best. However, SMM can become expensive if you do not clearly understand how to do it effectively. For instance, you will spend money on paid advertisements that do little to attract the attention of potential customers.

Each social media platform has different rules for success. Nevertheless, there is one thing that is common if you want to run a successful SMM campaign- consistency. This goes right back to creating a strong content marketing plan that will serve as a guide for all your digital marketing efforts. It is not as simple as creating an account, putting up a few posts and hoping for the best.

It is also important to link your website to your social media accounts. Your social media accounts can include links that direct people to content on your website. Your website's blog should include social media sharing options to give your content more exposure. The link between your social media profiles and your website should be seamless.

This is not a marketing guide so we will not delve into the nuances of successful SMM on each platform here. However, there are a wide range of books that cover the topic. I have found that Alan Dib's book "The 1-Page Marketing Plan" has helped me with digital marketing in general, but it also contains some useful information about using social media to your advantage. I highly recommend that you read this book.

Email Marketing

An email subscriber list is marketing gold. Most digital marketing experts agree that it is best to spend time building an email subscriber list since these subscribers would have already expressed interest in your product or service. They have already gone through the first stage of the sales funnel.

Email marketing is all about maintaining the interest of your email subscriber list and taking them down the sales funnel until they become paying customers. The most popular online email marketing platform is MailChimp, but there are other platforms such as:

- Constant Contact
- Get Response
- Convert Kit
- Mailer Lite
- Zoho Campaigns

A successful email marketing campaign should have:

- Subscriber lists grouped according to business segments and personalized needs.
- A different campaign for each subscriber list.
- An understanding of user preferences.
- Email automation for customers at each stage of the sales funnel.
- A catchy email subject.
- A clear call to action.

Your website is a good way to build your email subscriber list. You may have visited a website recently that asked you to subscribe to their mailing list so that you could get special deals and discounts. Another website may have asked you to subscribe so that you could download free content. Various websites use different strategies to increase the number of email subscribers.

It is best to hire a professional to ensure that your email marketing campaign is done right. The Success Lifestyle Magazine team can help you create and execute an email marketing campaign that produces results. Contact us at info@successlifestylemagazine.com for more information.

Are traditional advertising strategies still relevant?

Yes, traditional advertising strategies are still relevant. According to an article published in the Jamaica Observer on May 1, 2018 entitled, "Jamaica third largest internet user base in the Caribbean", 56 percent of Jamaicans had access to the internet in 2018. That means that there is still 44 percent of the population that does not have internet access. Traditional advertising helps you reach both groups. In fact, it acts as reinforcement for people who may have seen something about your brand online.

Traditional advertising includes radio ads, television ads, print ads, billboards and direct mailing. Like digital marketing, you must have a clear plan to achieve your goals with traditional advertising. You may need to hire a local advertising professional to help you do this. Just know that traditional advertising is not dead and should be included in your overall marketing campaign especially if your brand focuses solely on the Jamaican audience.

Key Points from Chapter 5

- Digital marketing and traditional advertising should both be a part of your marketing strategy.

- Any marketing campaign you embark on should have SMARTER goals.

- Your marketing budget should be about 8 percent of your revenue, but you should watch your campaigns closely to ensure that you are not overspending.

- An email subscriber list is a highly valuable marketing tool.

- Some elements of marketing you can learn yourself, but it is better to hire a professional to avoid making costly mistakes.

- A website is your brand's online real estate and is the focal point of all your digital marketing efforts.

Checklist

- ☐ Create a website.

- ☐ Use SEO best practices throughout the website.

- ☐ Create a blog on the website.

- ☐ Create a content marketing plan for all your digital platforms.

- ☐ Implement the content marketing plan and hire professionals as necessary.

- ☐ Determine the types of traditional advertising that are necessary for your business and hire a professional to help you make these ads happen.

Reflection Question

What marketing strategy do you need to use for your business?
How will you implement it?

_____

_____

_____

_____

_____

_____

_____

_____

_____

_____

_____

_____

_____

_____

_____

_____

_____

Chapter Seven: *Fear Need Fi Dash Weh*

There is a popular quote from Zig Ziglar that is particularly poignant when engaging in any discussion about fear. It says, "Fear has two meanings: forget everything and run or face everything and rise. The choice is yours." You have probably heard it before, and it may make you feel like being fearful is wrong. You may even be saying, "Christine, you don't understand how hard it is to face fear and rise above it. You have no idea what I'm going through!" I actually do.

I fear many things. This may seem silly but there was a period in my life when I feared talking to people on the phone; my heart would race each time I made a phone call. What if the person is busy and does not want to talk to me? What if I do not say the right thing? I would find any way to either get someone else to make the call or send the person a text message. I believe that this fear prevented me from strengthening some important relationships. Thankfully, it is a fear that I have faced and risen above.

Deciding to pursue entrepreneurship is both exhilarating and frightening. The exhilaration comes from the possibility of experiencing financial freedom while pursuing your passion. But then there is the fear that creeps up on you like a shadow lurking in the dark. This fear comes from uncertainty about the unknown. Several questions start popping up in your mind:

- Will this work?
- What if I fail?
- Who am I to think that I can create something successful?
- What if my money runs out?
- What happens if I risk everything only to be left in the mud?
- How will I take care of those who depend on me?
- What if I am not good enough for this?

Entrepreneurship is risky. There is no doubt about that. The possibility of failure will always exist, but there is also the possibility of success. The risk is worth the reward. Can you handle it? Here are some tips that can help you answer this question with a resounding, "Yes!".

Reframe Failure

The first step to conquer fear is to reframe failure. Be honest. How does your thinking change the moment you experience failure? One or more of these thoughts probably cross your mind:

- I cannot do this.

- I am stupid.

- I will never get this right.

The problem with these statements is that they are all negative and they make failure seem final. Perspective is a hell of a thing. Consider how a positive perspective could help you reframe the 3 negative thoughts previously mentioned. You could say instead:

- I can do this. Sure, I made a few mistakes, but I have learned something from them.

- I am smart and capable. What sets me apart from others is how quickly I can learn from the experience, get myself back on my feet and move forward.

- I can master this. It was only on attempt 1,001 that Thomas Edison was able to successfully create the light bulb.

Putting a positive spin on failure requires some rewiring of your brain. You may have already programmed your brain to respond negatively each time there is the faintest hint of failure. However, this does not mean that you cannot use all of the following strategies to rewire your brain so that you can think positively.

Strategy #1: Flip negatives into positives.

You hear the negative thought forming in your head. Instead of letting it fester like an open wound, put a positive spin on it. That was what I did earlier when I reframed the three negative thoughts into positive thoughts. Here is another example.

You have taken a job that is slightly difficult but something you know you can do. You give it your all, but the stress of the job and your life causes you to respond harshly to the client unintentionally. As a result, a potential long-term relationship is cut short. You start thinking, "How could I be so stu…" but then shift your thinking to, "I am going to learn how to control my responses so that I do not ruin client relationships." A perspective shift gives you a solution to help you move forward.

Strategy #2: Begin and end each day with a sense of gratitude.

Reframing failure is all about developing a habit of positivity. It helps to wake up each day with a heart of gratitude because that positive energy permeates throughout the rest of the day. Therefore, you should begin each day by identifying at least one thing for which you can be grateful.

At the end of the day, just before you put your head on your pillow to rest, take some time to reflect. Some days are challenging, but that does not mean that there is not something positive that you can reflect on. What lessons did you learn? What is the simplest thing that happened that brought a smile to your face? What was the best part of the day?

Strategy #3: Do something nice for someone each day.

Acts of kindness release endorphins, the "feel good" hormones. We can often feel like being kind to others is pointless. People are ungrateful and will probably trample all over you if they get the chance. At least that is what we believe our experiences and society have taught us.

Look at it this way. Being kind is more about what you can do to help others be their best selves rather than about what you can get in return. The late Mother Teresa summed it up nicely. She said,

People are often unreasonable, illogical and self-centered;
Forgive them anyway.

If you are kind, people may accuse you of selfish, ulterior motives;
Be kind anyway.

If you are successful, you will win some false friends and some true enemies;
Succeed anyway.

If you are honest and frank, people may cheat you;
Be honest and frank anyway.

What you spend years building, someone could destroy overnight;
Build anyway.

If you find serenity and happiness, they may be jealous;
Be happy anyway.

The good you do today, people will often forget tomorrow;

Do good anyway.

Give the world the best you have, and it may never be enough;
Give the world the best you've got anyway.

You see, in the final analysis, it is between you and your God;
It was never between you and them anyway.

The lesson? Do good anyway.

Strategy #4: Do not downplay your feelings.

It would be unfair to say that you should ignore fear and all the emotions that accompany it. Acknowledge that the fear you experience is real. Understand the emotions you feel when fear creeps up on you. Developing this self-awareness means that you will be able to keep your emotions in check and respond positively.

Know Your Triggers

You must first know what your trigger is before you can rectify it. In this context, a trigger is a thought or action that causes you to respond with fear. Think of it like a gun's trigger;

press on it and a bullet is released. Pulling the trigger unleashes sometimes irreparable damage.

All emotions have triggers, but those triggers differ from one person to the next. For instance, a person with a fear of spiders (arachnophobia) is triggered by the sight of a spider. The trigger for the fear that is preventing you from pursuing your business dreams may not be as simple to identify.

This trigger often relates to the areas of our lives where we feel unsatisfied. Some possibilities include:

- Seeing a social media post of a successful entrepreneur and wondering, "Why can't I be like her?"
- Looking at the lives of those around you and feeling like you are far behind.
- Engaging with someone or something that goes against your ideals and firmly held beliefs.
- Remembering a volatile period in your life that made you feel belittled, insignificant and incapable.

Some of these triggers are deep and have no quick fix. You do not want to put a Band-Aid on a wound that requires deep healing. Accept the fact that it may take months or years before you can adequately deal with your fear trigger. You may need to consult a psychologist or psychiatrist for additional support if that fear trigger runs deep.

However, some fear triggers can be addressed through a shift in mindset. In fact, this may be a good place to start before seeking professional help. For instance, if your fear is triggered by envy you can condition your mind to focus on your own success path rather than compare yourself with others. Changing the way, you think is the key to handling your fear trigger.

Common Fears Experienced by New Entrepreneurs

Fear is a natural part of the process towards becoming an entrepreneur. Even those entrepreneurs who seem strong and confident have battled with their fears behind closed doors. The entrepreneurial journey will test every aspect of your mental well-being. Here are seven of the most common fears faced by new entrepreneurs.

Fear #1: No one will want the product or service.

You are taking a great risk by transforming your skills and passions into a business. The fact that these are products or services that you believe in does not mean that others will feel the same way. Your market research may have given you mixed responses that make it even more challenging to determine if this business venture will succeed. Sure, you have the right to wonder what will happen if people do not want your product or service. However, what will happen if they do?

I remember having a conversation with Fiona Lyn-Johnston, founder and CEO of Sculpted Memories Casting Studio, that centred on this fear. She is very creative and had been dabbling in various creative ventures over the years with a small measure of success. She knew that she was passionate about making beautiful casts as keepsakes for precious memories. However, her idea was something completely new to the Jamaican market and she felt that it would not work. Her family and I encouraged her to press on; she did and her business is growing. Who knew that Jamaicans would love sculpted memories?

You will not know if your business idea can work unless you take the risk. Understand that it will take hard work, sacrifice and commitment. You will also need a community of support that consists of people who motivate you, loyal customers and investors. It will take a while to build this community. Nevertheless, the community, your hard work and your dedication will help your business succeed in the long-term.

Fear #2: The business will be a money pit and consume all my finances.

Chapter four covered the importance of proper financial planning to ensure that your business' financial needs are covered, especially if you are bootstrapping. The reality is though that life is unpredictable, and we live in an imperfect market. You could have everything planned to the T but have a spontaneous event take you by surprise.

Therefore, it is important for you to be strategic with your planning. Always have a backup plan. For instance, Plan A will always be to ensure that you have a rainy-day fund and have enough money saved to cover your expenses for at least the first 3 months after leaving your 9 to 5. Plan B would need to cover the actions you will take if those funds dry up before they should. How will you get your business to a place where it can be financially stable?

Fear #3: Your business will not remain innovative and will fall to the back of the pack.

Your creative energy is at its peak when you are just starting a business. You are actively paying attention to what is happening in the market and trying to do everything possible to make your business unique. You are ready with guns blazing, nothing can stop you now!

But what happens when your business matures? How will it remain innovative? How will it increase market share? Will it be doomed to fail? These are powerful questions and the answer to them is two-fold. Firstly, lifelong learning must be your priority. Secondly, the team you hire must be committed to lifelong learning and innovation; they must share your vision of creating a company that always stays ahead of the game.

Fear #4: You will outgrow the company.

Our objectives at each stage of life change as time progresses. A company that you may have been passionate about in your 20s may not be a company that you are passionate about in your 40s. Be prepared to transition into other business endeavours as you age. Give your best to the company that you are starting now so that is at the top of its game when it is time for you to leave.

Fear #5: You do not have all the skills to run a successful company.

Entrepreneurship is a continuous learning experience. There are some people who have innate business skills, but that does not mean that you cannot learn how to become a successful entrepreneur. The time will never be ***right*** for you to start your business because you will always feel that there is something missing. Steve Jobs did not think about whether it was the right time to start Apple, he just did it.

Fear #6: Your business will take you away from your family.

This fear cuts deep. Running a business, especially during the startup years, is time consuming. You will probably be working 18 hours per day and spending little time with the ones you love. Chances are they will not understand why you are not spending enough time with them and they may become resentful. The result? You feel more pressure added to the stress that is already on your plate.

Striking a healthy work-life balance will be challenging. However, it is necessary for your physical, spiritual, mental and emotional well-being. Here are some tips to help you strike a healthy work-life balance despite your demanding schedule:

- Focus on your strengths and outsource the rest to others. Trying to be a Jack of all Trades is part of the reason you never have enough time.

- Simplify your daily task list. Your daily task list should not have more than 5 items and they should be arranged in order of priority.

- Deliberately include personal time in your daily schedule, even if it is only an hour. This also applies to family time.

- Set aside one night each week as date night for you and your spouse. Do not look at it as a chore. Instead, use it as an opportunity to disengage from work and give your spouse your undivided attention.

Fear #7: Your business will affect your health.

Entrepreneurs are known to have an array of health problems ranging from depression to coronary artery disease. We often use lack of time as an excuse to eat unhealthy food and ignore our mental health. Do not fall into that trap. Healthy eating is expensive in Jamaica but it is possible, even on a tight budget, if you:

- Do not use frying as a cooking technique. Baking, roasting or grilling works.

- Avoid fast food as much as possible. If you can reduce your fast food intake to once per month then you have accomplished something great.

- Cook ground provisions instead of rice. Rice and peas is Jamaica's unofficial second national dish. We tend to eat it daily without question. Too much a one ting nuh good fi yuh.

- Include vegetables and fruits in your diet. They are expensive but try to start by at least having fruits and vegetables three times per week.

- Only drink water. Sodas and other sugary beverages are not good for you.

It is also important for exercise to become routine. Few people love to exercise. It is hard. It hurts. It makes you sweat like a dog. However, it is necessary for your physical health. You may not have the money to join a gym and hire a personal trainer, but the internet offers several home workout options. Some possible home workout options on YouTube are:

- Pop Sugar Fitness
- Tone It Up
- Fitness Blender
- The Fitness Marshall

Stop Letting Fear Hold You Back

You have so much to offer this world. Stop letting fear hold you back. Risk-takers do not have easy lives, but they do not live a life of regret. Only you have control over your life and your actions. Stop blaming your lack of commitment and follow-through on others. Shake off the fear and step into a chance for entrepreneurial success.

Key Points from Chapter 7

- Fear is a real emotion. Do not apologize for feeling it but learn how to deal with it.

- Fear is a natural part of an entrepreneur's journey. Learn to conquer it through the power of a positive mindset.

- Do not allow entrepreneurship to consume your life. Outsource tasks that you struggle with and make a deliberate effort to spend time with the ones you love.

- Do not neglect your overall well-being in pursuit of success.

- Always have a strategy in place to cover worst case scenarios.

- Speak with a professional if you have some deeply rooted fears that are connected to volatile periods in your life.

Checklist

- ☐ Make positive thinking a habit.
- ☐ Create a strategic plan for starting your business that covers all possible outcomes.
- ☐ Schedule a session with a professional if you have deeply rooted fears.
- ☐ Create and implement a health and wellness plan to cover your holistic wellbeing.

☐ Outsource tasks that would be better done by others.

☐ Create a more realistic daily schedule.

Reflection Questions

What is the biggest fear that you need to overcome? How will you overcome it?

_____

_____

_____

_____

_____

_____

_____

_____

_____

_____

_____

_____

_____

_____

_____

_____

_____

_____

_____

Chapter Eight: *Rome Neva Buil' Inna A Day*

Rome is an architectural marvel. It is known for the awe-inspiring Colosseum, Pantheon, Baths of Caracalla and Temple of Bacchus. Look them up! They truly are gorgeous ancient masterpieces. Such beautiful architecture takes several years to complete. In fact, it took six to eight *years* for the Romans to build the Colosseum. Building a masterpiece takes time. The gorgeous Roman empire could not have been built in a day.

The same concept can be transferred to creating a successful business. It will take years for your business to evolve into a beautiful masterpiece. A wide range of fears were discussed in chapter seven. Mention was made of the fear of your business losing its ability to be innovative. It is a concerning fear because lack of innovation results in a business falling behind its competitors and ultimately fading into obscurity. However, it is important to be mindful of the fact that innovation requires growth and your company has to be prepared for growth. In other words, it is important to always stay ahead of the game, but it is also important to prepare your business for the next phase of growth when you decide to incorporate new business processes and products.

How to Prepare Your Business for Growth

1. Determine if your business is ready for growth.

Preparing for growth is an ongoing process so that you and your team are ready when a growth opportunity becomes evident. However, you should develop the ability to identify whether your business is ready for growth. Here are some key factors that you should note:

- You are getting more customers than you can handle.
- The industry is evolving.
- You have strong cash flow.
- Business goals are being accomplished.
- The business is bursting at the seams in its current location.

Some entrepreneurs expand their businesses too soon. Do not fall into the same trap. The most important factors to consider from the list above are an increase in customers, strong cash flow and business goals being accomplished. You will need cash flow to expand but the expansion won't make sense if there is no customer demand. Additionally, your business will face challenges if your team is not able to meet the current business goals. How will they cope when these goals become increasingly challenging during and after the expansion?

2. **Have a growth plan.**

There should be a clear vision of where you want the company to be in five, ten and even twenty years. This vision forms your growth plan and it is an element that can be included in your business plan. The growth plan details what the business will look like a few years later and how the business will get there. It should include:

- A year-by-year goal that takes the business closer to that growth objective
- A 12-month schedule that facilitates the annual goal
- Outcomes of quarterly revisions
- Opportunities for key players to meet daily or weekly to check on the progress

The growth plan is not something that you should develop alone. Invite your team to be a part of the process. People are more likely to accept something that they have helped develop.

3. Invest in your team.

A happy and committed team can help your business grow in leaps and bounds. Your team is your most valuable resource. You may not be able to hire a human resource manager, but this is a role that you should take on as the leader of the business. Here are some important ways to invest in your team and show that you care about them:

- Show that you value family. For instance, do not let it be a problem if a working mother needs to leave work a bit early to deal with an emergency with her child. Also, allow your team to leave work at the end of work hours so that they can be with their families. The team will become resentful if it seems like work is all you care about.

- Pay for the team to attend local and international conferences so that they can stay ahead of the game.

- Sponsor a staff member furthering his or her education. You may not be able to grant a scholarship, but you can at least offer a loan at a very low interest rate.

- Plan and engage in fun team building activities.
- Celebrate personal achievements.
- Acknowledge the efforts of your team members, even if you just say, "Thank you".
- Reward and publicly recognize good work.

3. Invest profits.

It is not uncommon for entrepreneurs to treat their business' finances like their personal finances. All the money earned is just thrown into a bank account. Saving is different from investing. It is important for you to have a business bank account that has money for recurring business expenses such as payroll, utility bills and paying suppliers. However, a portion of the business' profits should be invested. You should invest in real estate, stocks, bonds, unit trusts or any other investment instrument that helps you gain reasonable returns.

4. Prepare your team for change.

The second point spoke about investing in your team which is something that should become a habit in your business. It is also important to prepare your team for change. Growth requires change and the transition can be difficult because we have an innate desire to resist change. Here are some strategies that you can use to prepare your team for change:

- Ensure that **all** team members clearly understand what is happening and why it is necessary. You need their buy-in if you want the change to be effective.

- Invite collaboration to flesh out the growth strategy and the way forward for the organization. Collaboration should be across teams in the business and not just within teams. For instance, the finance department should collaborate with the marketing department.

- Ensure that all teams have a competitive edge and are performing at their optimal level.

- Develop a spirit of problem solving and critical thinking.

5. Prepare your infrastructure.

Infrastructure includes both your business' physical location and technology. You will need to invest in upgrades and changes that reflect the growth objective. If you start investing in these upgrades early enough, they will not become burdensome when it is time to facilitate a transition for growth.

Be a Lifelong Learner

Entrepreneurship is a constant learning experience. Whether you are the only person in your business, or you are working with a team, you should make continuous learning a habit. Your business will be better off when you take the time to gain more knowledge and experience.

It is quite possible that you will not have the time to adopt conventional lifelong learning habits during the early stages of your business. You will be working long hours and have little, if any, time for yourself. Nevertheless, it is important for you to find calm in the mayhem. The most successful entrepreneurs adopt the following lifelong learning habits:

- Spend less than 2 hours a day watching television.
- Spend at least an hour each day reading books and other material related to your industry.
- Spend at least an hour each day mastering your craft.
- Watch or read local or international news daily.

- Listen to podcasts while commuting. These podcasts can be industry or personal development related.

- Read at least 1 personal development book per month.

- Attend at least 1 industry related conference per year.

- Upgrade your skills by furthering your education.

The Race is not for the Swift

A common thread running through this book is a clear understanding that entrepreneurship is not simple. There are 5 soft skills that you should develop if you are committed to being a successful entrepreneur. These skills take time to develop so do not be too hard on yourself if some are easier for you to develop than others.

Soft Skill #1: Self-regulation

Entrepreneurship is a true test of patience. You will be dealing with people who have diverse backgrounds, opinions and personalities. They will think and behave differently from you. There are times when you will feel frustrated and want to respond in an unprofessional way. This is where self-regulation becomes pivotal.

It is not worth responding unprofessionally and losing a valuable team member or customer. Be aware of how you are feeling and take some time to calm down before responding. Practice empathy without allowing others to take advantage of your kindness. Think before you act.

Soft Skill #2: Effective Communication Skills

A good entrepreneur understands that communication is not only about getting his or her message across. Active listening is also important and is something that you should do with both your team members and customers. We can sometimes become too caught up in our thoughts and feelings that we forget to listen to and appreciate another perspective. Here are some steps for active communication:

- Give the other person your undivided attention. Put down the phone. Make eye contact. Stop thinking about the next point that you want to raise.
- Ask clarifying questions to ensure that you understand.
- Do not be judgmental. Listen objectively.

- Respond calmly and appropriately.

It is also important for your instructions to be as clear as possible for your team members. A lot of time can be wasted when a team member does not understand what you have requested and, therefore, presents the wrong output. If you are sending instructions via email or other electronic media, include a sentence or 2 that provides the options for the team member to seek further clarification if necessary.

Soft Skill #3: The ability to be amicable

People will not do business with someone they do not like. Similarly, people will not want to work with a boss who is a pain in the ass. It does not matter if you are an introvert, you should get along with others if you want to succeed in the business world. Care about other people and be friendly enough to make them feel comfortable. Granted, not everyone will be your cup of tea and personalities will clash it it is still important for you to be likeable

Soft Skill #4: Problem Solving

Your business was created to solve a problem in the market… to fill a need. This does not mean that the problems are only outside the business. You will face a lot of internal problems, especially as the business develops. Problem solving should become second nature. You will need to think quickly on your feet and deal with problems that you have never previously faced.

Soft Skill #5: The ability to inspire others

Successful entrepreneurs are strong leaders. The ability to inspire is crucial for leadership. Your team should respect you and be inspired by who you are and the vision you have for the company. Inspiration is something intangible that cannot be demanded or forced. It is something that evolves over time as your team gets to know you and builds trust in you.

Key Points from Chapter 8

- Your business should always be prepared for growth.

- Taking on a new venture or expanding your business is something you should avoid if your business is not ready for growth.

- Successful entrepreneurs are lifelong learners.

- There are 5 fundamental soft skills that all entrepreneurs should possess

Checklist

- ☐ Create a growth plan.

- ☐ Create more opportunities for staff to increase their knowledge and experience.

- ☐ Change your daily life so that you can make lifelong learning a habit.

- ☐ Determine the soft skills that you need to develop and work on them.

Reflection Question

What changes do you need to make for business and personal success?

_____

_____

_____

_____

_____

_____

_____

_____

_____

_____

_____

_____

_____

_____

_____

_____

_____

References

1. 47 chronically delinquent taxpayers arrested in St. Ann (2019, July 23). *The Gleaner.* Retrieved from http://jamaica-gleaner.com/article/news/20190723/47-chronically-delinquent-taxpayers-arrested-st-ann-0.

2. Bennett, K. (2019, July 5). Update: Lenders aiming for $100b of loans to SMEs. *The Gleaner.* Retrieved from http://jamaica-gleaner.com/article/business/20190705/update-lenders-aiming-100b-loans-smes.

3. Clarke, C. (2019). How to start your business with help from the JBDC. Success Lifestyle Magazine, 4, 12-14.

4. EXIM Bank Jamaica (n.d.). EXIM Bank Today. Retrieved from http://www.eximbankja.com/about.

5. Graham, N. (2019, March 8). Santa Clarke- tax cuts, duty abolition to spark $14b stimulus package. *The Gleaner.* Retrieved from http://jamaica-gleaner.com/article/lead-stories/20190308/santa-clarke-tax-cuts-duty-abolition-spark-14b-stimulus-package.

6. Jamaica Business Development Corporation. Who we are. Retrieved from https://www.jbdc.net/.

7. St. Catherine business persons arrested for failure to pay taxes (2015). Retrieved from https://www.jamaicatax.gov.jm/home/-/blogs/st-catherine-business-persons-arrested-for-failure-to-pay-taxes.

8. St. Elizabeth businessman arrested for failure to file tax returns tax administration Jamaica's (TAJ) (n.d.). Retrieved from https://mof.gov.jm/mof-media/media-centre/press/2421-st-elizabeth-businessman-arrested-for-failure-to-file-tax-returns-tax-administration-jamaica-s-taj.html.

9. Tax Administration of Jamaica (n.d.). Forms. Retrieved from https://www.jamaicatax.gov.jm/forms

10. The Companies Office of Jamaica (n.d.). Online Business Registration. Retrieved from https://www.orcjamaica.com/

11. The Development Bank of Jamaica (n.d.). Services. Retrieved from https://dbankjm.com/services/